ReWrite

THE JOURNEY FROM SELF-HARM TO HEALING

BENJAMIN SLEDGE

HeartSupport, Inc.
PO Box 19461
Austin, TX 78760
info@heartsupport.com
www.heartsupport.com

For Leanna
Who was brave enough to bare
her scars and soul.

CONTENTS

INTRODUCTION

One of the first moments of crisis we had at our organization occurred when a girl named Leanna and a young man named Stephan reached out for help because they were chronic self-injurers.

HeartSupport got its start by providing relevant recovery for an online generation, but self-harm wasn't initially one of our focuses. Our founder, Jake Luhrs, is the lead singer for the Grammy-nominated metal band August Burns Red, and while praying outside a House of Blues one evening, he knew he had to do something to change the trajectory of his fans with the platform he'd been given.

Each night after a show, fans would come up and share their stories of addiction, pain, broken relationships, or thoughts of suicide. So when we began, self-harm was a minor blip on our radar compared to where our attention was focused. Little did we know that self-harm among our community would become a driving force behind our recovery efforts for men and women.

Initially, none of the volunteers or team members had any experience with self-harm (often called cutting) when Stephan and Leanna reached out. We didn't understand why people would cut themselves, especially since humans have a fight-or-flight response when experiencing pain. It made little sense to us. Personally, I didn't even know what self-harm was. Later, I would discover that self-harm was defined as "hurting yourself on purpose," and while the techniques and tactics of how people hurt themselves varies, most I encountered inflicted cuts on their arms or thighs using razor blades or knives. Many would cut over a period of months and years.

It was then my eyes opened. The revelation was like a movie scene in which you discover an underworld of people you didn't know existed or got invited to a thriving underground casino. When I began openly talking about the subject, friends would come forward and admit they'd self-injured in the past.

The more we dealt with the issue at HeartSupport, the more we studied and learned effective techniques and tactics to help people break free. We also discovered a lot of stigmas and callous thinking from the populace at large.

We would hear about how self-injurers were "pussies" who couldn't cope with life. Nurses would tell men and women who ended up in the hospital they better get right with Jesus before they end up dead or in an insane asylum. Parents would ground their children and proclaim that, back in their day, this kind of thing never happened.

Is it any wonder the world of self-injury has remained hidden for so long when to even hint at it would mean ridicule?

As awareness about self-harm has grown, so has the

need for resources. Unfortunately, most books on the subject read like a medical thesaurus with terms we had a difficult time grasping. Other times, the information seemed contradictory as far as how to help. Were these suicide attempts? *The answer is generally no.* Was this a mental illness? *Well, sort of, it's behavioral.*

What began as an experiment turned into a book. This book. We asked men and women online if they'd be willing to talk to us about their experience with self-harm. We had over 300 different responses. Many of the voices you hear in this book came from our online community, reaching out to us. We have quoted them but have preserved their privacy and identity.

At that point, we knew we had to create a clear and concise book that was not only relevant, but easy to understand. We didn't want it to just be information people digested either. There had to be action and a learning environment where people could experience recovery in the manner they understood. Some people are auditory learners, some visual, and some tactile. When this book started to come along, we decided to tackle all three.

How do we intend to do that in a book you may ask?

First, you will learn about the who, what, and why behind self-harm. We want you to become educated about everything from recovery tactics to relapse. At the end of each chapter, there will be a link you can enter into a computer browser or phone that will recap and provide a case study of a young woman named Victoria who broke free from self-harm.

Finally, once you're done reading, you will have the opportunity to put what you've learned into practice.

There will be journaling and workbook exercises to help you begin the healing process.

If you're a friend or family member of someone who self-harms, this book is for you too. Not only will you learn from the perspective of your loved one, but there are even sections and chapters to show the best means to help.

Whether you've been injuring for years or a few days, are male or female, married or single, teenager or senior, I can promise you that packed within these pages are words that will speak to the depths or your soul. Some of our early reviewers said, "Finally! FINALLY! Something I can share with others so they can understand how I feel."

We at HeartSupport hope and pray this book does the same for you.

1

THE MIDDLE,

Where Everything Looks Like Failure
(But It's Not)

Those who have been in the chamber of affliction know how to comfort those who are there. Do not believe that any man will become a physician unless he walks the hospitals; and I am sure that no one will become a divine, or become a comforter, unless he lies in the hospital as well as walks through it, and has to suffer himself.
—Charles Spurgeon

"I cut too deep last night…I almost had to go to the hospital." I can hear the strain in her voice as she struggles to tell me. I try to be encouraging, but she sounds more like the person who's reached the end of their rope. And it appears there's nothing I can do about it.

For months, Leanna and I have talked, and her situation is only getting worse. She's hiding bloody rags under her bed. Her family and friends know nothing. She wears hoodies and long sleeves in the middle of summer to hide her scars. She hates herself, and I, well, I hate myself too because I can't do anything to stop it.

We're both tired, both want to give up, and if our lives were a Vietnam War movie we'd be soaked in napalm and left to burn. We're losing the war, except there's no exit plan or surrender. Just defeat. She's giving up and I'm losing hope.

Everything looks like failure.

If you're someone struggling with self-harm, this might be exactly how you feel. No progress, and no way out. If you're a friend, parent, or loved one of someone struggling with self-harm, then maybe you too feel at a loss for what to do or how to help.

Regardless of where you find yourself walking into this—even if you're reading this as that last-ditch effort—you are not beyond hope. You're just in the middle of your journey, and the middle always feels like failure.

For the patient who has cancer and is going through chemo, their reality is they still have cancer. For the young man, or young woman cutting and depressed, their reality is they're still cutting. For the guy or girl running a marathon who hits a wall at mile 13 and decides they can't go on, they've realized they have thirteen more miles to go.

Everything looks like failure in the middle. But the middle isn't the ending. The middle is actually what makes the ending much more beautiful.

The young girl, Leanna, who was also referenced in the Introduction and whose story I began with, was cutting because she was being sex trafficked. She was just sixteen.

As you'll come to find out, however, there are numerous reasons why men and women cut themselves. But the middle of Leanna's story was not her ending. Today, at age twenty-one, she is free from self-harm and works for an organization fighting against human trafficking and sex slavery.

I began with the quote from Spurgeon because HeartSupport walks with people daily through numerous issues (self-harm being chief among them). We've walked through the proverbial hospitals, and much of this book is made with the help of those who've at one point been inside that "hospital."

Inside this book and the accompanying video programs, you'll find advice and help from over 300 people who've walked through self-harm and come out clean. If we were to add up the sum of their experiences, we'd have an average of over 2,400 years of experience and recovery.

We hope you'll take this journey with us seriously and complete the exercises. Don't stay stuck in the middle.

Your ending is still being written.

To watch the accompanying videos that recap the chapter and provide a case study, visit http:// heartsupport.com/SH

2

THE WHAT

(and Let's Clear Up the Stigmas Surrounding Self-Harm)

Have you ever played a card game called Taboo? Lots of families play it together. If you're not familiar with the game, the goal is for one player to pick up a card and get their team to guess the word on that card. The trick is they have to give clues without using the word itself or five additional "taboo" words listed on the card.

Imagine you were playing the game, and you picked up the card with the word *self-harm*. You immediately knew how you would describe it to get your team to guess it, but then you glance down, and you see the words you can't use are *razor blade, goth, cutting, black clothes,* and *emo.* So how would you describe self-harm? Would it even be possible to describe self-harm without those descriptors?

While most people immediately imagine the stereotypical young teenager in goth clothing who's cutting themselves on the arm with a razor blade, this is hardly the full scope of what self-harm is.

The National Alliance on Mental Illness describes

self-harm or self-injury as a "means of hurting yourself on purpose." The most common and well-known way to do so is cutting yourself with a sharp object (such as a razor blade or knife), but encompasses a wide range of behaviors. Some people scratch themselves with wire coat hangers. Others will burn themselves or even put cigarettes out on their body. Sometimes they even write words like *loser* or *worthless* into their arms and legs.

The behavior can range from hitting body parts to breaking bones, compulsive skin picking to allow wounds the inability to heal, hair pulling, or even ingesting toxic substances or objects (not including alcohol or mood-altering substances).

At this point you may be wondering just why you started self-injury, maybe you know, or maybe as a parent or friend you'd like to understand what caused this behavior. I'll discuss that more in chapter 3, but for now let's address a few stigmas.

BREAKING DOWN THE STIGMAS

While I'm not a parent, I know my mother was equally perplexed as she was concerned about my self-harm. [To her] it didn't seem to make sense. The greatest thing that my family could have done during that time was to listen without judgment. Their intervention, their questions, their pleading did little to change the way I felt, and it certainly didn't make me feel better. What I needed to know was that I had a safety net with them so that no matter where I was in my recovery, they would be there. —Ashley

Stigma 1: They're Doing It for Attention

Each year our team heads out on Vans Warped Tour and spends countless hours talking to adults, millennials, teenagers, and parents. We see young men and women wearing black hoodies in the middle of a Texas summer. Others will be in long sleeves and pants, knowing full well the event is outdoors and the temperature will reach 101 degrees. Others wear wristbands that practically climb their arm to the base of their elbow.

Is this just a fashion trend?

No. The vast majority of those wearing these outfits are covering their scars or recently inflicted wounds. They don't want anyone to know what they're doing because of one simple truth: They're ashamed they cut.

According to the research of Dr. Michael Hollander, a nationally recognized expert on self-injury, less than 4 percent of those who self-harm do so for attention. Yet many college and high school counselors, therapists, or parents will wrongly attribute the behavior as a cry for attention.

Think back to when you first started cutting or discovered a friend or loved one was cutting.

- How long had you been doing it?
- How long before someone else found out?
- How long until you realized your friend or child was self-injuring?

The most common answer is "months or years," maybe

even "never." Many who self-harm do so in secret out of a deep sense of shame that someone would find out and judge them or ostracize their behavior.

Stigma 2: Self-Harm Is a Trend

Self-harm is actually quite ancient. In antiquity the behavior was most often used in religious practices. One of the earliest incidents we have recorded is in the Old Testament Biblical narrative where the prophets of Baal cut themselves in honor of their god to force him into action (the event is recorded in 1st Kings 18:26–28, but doesn't end well for the prophets).

Later, the practice of self-flagellation took hold in the Roman Catholic Church where practitioners would whip themselves as an extreme form of religious devotion. Various religions, like the cult of Isis in Egypt and the Dionysian cult of Greece, practiced their own forms of flagellation. In ancient Rome, eunuch priests of the Phrygian goddess Cybele, the Galli, flogged themselves until they bled during the annual festival called Dies Sanguinis (Day of Blood). To this day some Shiite Muslims practice self-flagellation, and in some traditional forms of Wicca there is the practice of "gentle scourging."

Also note that animals in the wild are also known to self-injure most often through the form of hair pulling. They will begin to obsessively groom themselves and inevitably groom their children. Perhaps more alarming is that the children often emulate the actions of the parents as a means to "self-sooth."

More important than the historical roots of self-harm, however, is the heart behind the claim that self-harm is a trend. When a parent or friend dismisses self-harm as "just a trend" or some kind of "fad" they'll grow out of, it belittles the emotional turmoil their loved one is experiencing. It assumes their loved one is naive. It says, "You're just following what you think other people are doing and what other people think is cool."

But the reality is this: regardless of how they were introduced to self-harm, they continue in this struggle because it offers them emotional relief from deeper difficulties they're facing. And by thinking self-harm is just a result of peer pressure, you're missing out on the opportunity to help this loved one find healing for their deep internal pain, and you're letting them sink into destructive external habits.

Stigma 3: They're Cutting Because They're Suicidal

Men and women who self-injure typically don't do so because they're suicidal. At HeartSupport we deal with people who are suicidal almost weekly, and the differentiation between someone who self-injures versus someone seeking to end their life is quite vast. While it's true that suicidal men and women can have problems with self-harm, you're just as likely (if not more) to find someone who wants to end their lives for a variety of reasons and has never injured themselves.

Many people have wrongly assumed self-injury is a failed or half-hearted suicide attempt. Remember, however, that many men and women self-harm in private. Those who are suicidal will almost always tell someone about it beforehand.

Humans' strongest drive is one of self-preservation, so

while some people may feel they want to die, part of them also wants to live. In some cases, self-injury is used as method of punishment to prevent suicide attempts.

> **Note for family and friends:** If you feel someone you know is suicidal in addition to their struggle with self-injury, it is imperative that they go through an assessment or seek professional help. You can even become certified online to spot the signs and refer appropriately. To become qualified in QPR (Question, Persuade, Refer), visit the QPR Institute at www.qprinstitute.com.

Stigma 4: They're Self-Harming Because They're Crazy and Need Hospitalization/Professional Help

Some people think that purposefully injuring yourself has to be the mind-set of someone who's obviously crazy and has mental issues (chapter 3 examines this issue in more depth).

It's a strange sentiment to hold considering many of us know at least one person who has struggled with alcohol, a Facebook friend who has an eating disorder, or a family member who is a workaholic. When we talk about destructive behavior and addictions in other realms like these, we often don't refer to that person as crazy because they've chosen a destructive coping mechanism.

Instead, we realize these people need help—not to be locked up in a hospital. While some do, in fact, need professional help or a rehab center, consider that many alcoholics recover, not through professional counseling, but by attending Alcoholics Anonymous with other addicts and through sponsors who have worked the 12 Steps. Many who have recovered from self-harm have done so specifically with the help of family members, friends, and other men and women who have struggled and found healing. More often than not, the wounds that are a result of self-injury do not require medical attention or become life threatening. Communicating to someone who self-injures that they're crazy can be potentially damaging and can compound feelings of guilt and shame (I'll talk more about that in chapter 4).

A psychologist who is an expert in the field of self-injury, Dr. Tracy Alderman explains the problem with hospitalization in her book *The Scarred Soul:*

> Fear can lead to dangerous overreactions. In dealing with clients who hurt themselves, you will probably feel fear…Hospitalizing clients for self-inflicted violence (SIV) is one such form of overreaction. Many therapists, because they do not possess an adequate understanding of SIV, will use extreme measures to assure (they think) their clients' best interests. However, few people who self-injure need to be hospitalized or institutionalized.…Hospitalizing a client involuntarily for these issues can be damaging in several ways. Because SIV is closely related to feelings of lack of control and overwhelming emotional states, placing someone in a setting that by its nature

evokes these feelings is very likely to make matters worse, and may lead to an incident of SIV.

In short, the person who is going to most impact someone who self-injures is the person who doesn't view them as crazy or mentally disturbed, but instead wants to understand, garner trust, and open effective lines of communication to help them overcome.

Stigma 5: Only Teenagers Do This—and They'll Grow Out of It

Self-injury can typically begin during the teenage years, but the myth that they're doing it for attention and will eventually grow out of such self-destructive behavior is simply that. A myth.

While it's true that life experience may help a teenager grow and learn new ways of coping with distress, it's important to note that simply getting older does not create emotional maturity. Even recent studies have coined a term known as *emerging adulthood* to show the recent delay in emotional maturation and coping skills as opposed to previous generations. Teenagers, and people in general, have to learn alternative methods to manage their emotions, which takes time, progress, and stable friends— which not everyone has.

In fact, a 2006 study in *Pediatrics* estimates that nearly one in five college students have deliberately injured themselves at least once. It should also be noted that when we surveyed over 300 men and women, many had injured well into their twenties, and others were still injuring despite being in their thirties.

Stigma 6: Only Emo, Goth, and Metalheads Self-injure

We hear this stigma often working in the music industry.

The metal and goth scene has long been associated with "devil worship" and mental health issues. Much of this scene, however, has been an outlet for men and women who felt like outcasts because of the style of music they enjoy. Because the style of music is often loud, emotional, and aggressive, many can wrongly assume that people who enjoy it are more inclined to aggressive forms of behavior.

While it's true that there are men and women who self-injure inside these music scenes, you're just as likely to find a large concentration of men and women who listen to Taylor Swift and self-harm. So should we conclude listening to Taylor Swift causes self-harm? No, that would be absurd. In fact, as you'll read in later chapters, self-harm affects people from all walks of life ranging from cheerleaders to parents to young professionals. There is no specific indicator in style of music or dress that pushes a demographic more toward self-harm than another.

WHO SELF-HARMS? JUST WOMEN?

A common misconception is that only women self-injure. During a study of self-injury among 5,000 Ivy League students, psychologist Janis Whitlock discovered that 20 percent of women surveyed injured, and 14 percent of men said they had injured at least once.

In fact, some 15 percent of teens are reporting some form of self-injury. Studies show an even higher risk for self-injury among college students, with rates ranging from 17 to 35 percent. In the United Kingdom, one in four young men are turning to self-harm as a result of anxiety, depression, and stress.

As you can see, the range is vast. Men and women from all backgrounds are injuring whether they're in the United States or abroad. Those we interviewed online ranged from teens to adults with children. Some were cheerleaders, some Ivy League students. They're the people you go to class with, meet at the club, go to church with, or stand next to in line for a movie. You just may not know it.

What's the reason for the vast increase in recent years of reported cases of self-injury?

Today's generation is faced with complex challenges their parents never experienced. Some 86 percent of eighteen-year-olds to twenty-nine-year-olds use social media, and 76 percent of them use it daily. People tend to post the highlights of their lives, which is why Instagram, among others, has become the new platform for lifestyle comparison.

As more social interaction is hosted online, it's easy for millennials to compare the unpolished aspects of their offline life to the filtered milestones of their friends' online life. Perhaps that's why 45 percent of college students say they feel hopeless, and 33 percent of millennials report looking for mental health resources online. Because of the growing need to compare their lives to one another, social media platforms are adding pressure and stress, and the skills needed to remain resilient aren't being taught.

Thus, men and women everywhere are looking for an outlet to cope or numb the constant need for approval.

But this is only one aspect why men and women are injuring themselves more readily.

Perhaps you're wondering exactly why they do it, and that's the subject of the next chapter.

To watch the accompanying videos that recap the chapter and provide a case study, visit http:// heartsupport.com/SH

3

THE WHY

(When Sometimes the Answer Is "Dunno")

Everyone has the same question: "Why?" Mostly, I just shrug my shoulders and mutter: "Dunno." I don't tell them that I am asking the same question of myself. I don't enjoy the process, nor do I like the scars. It's shameful and embarrassing. I desperately wanted to stop, but one thing kept getting in my way: after I cut, I felt better.
—Carrie Arnold

Imagine shopping at a mall where every cash register attendant was required to ask you why you were making that particular purchase. How would you answer?

Sometimes you'd say, "Because something's broken, and I need this hammer to fix it." Other times, you'd say, "Because I'm having a bad day, and buying these jeans will make my day better." Or perhaps in another example, you'd reply, "Because buying this pint of ice cream will help me forget about my breakup, my angry boss, my stress."

You could give a different answer to that question 365 days of the year. But there's something fundamentally similar to every answer you give: they all make sense to you in that moment.

Think about it: the joy of a new pair of jeans or a new gadget never lasts forever. Most of the items you buy replace items that you previously bought thinking it'd offer that same kind of lasting happiness. But in the moment when you're feeling sad or drained or bored and you need a pick-me-up, all that matters is that buying something will make you feel better right then and there. Sometimes it's not even a sensible purchase, but what matters is the emotional relief that item offers in the moment.

Even if you don't use retail therapy, you could use TV, food, pornography, tobacco, alcohol, or any number of outlets to make yourself feel better when you're not at your best. Self-harm, at its core, taps into the exact same logic. We'll dive into specific examples of what that might sound like for someone who self-harms, but it's important to know this: in the moment when someone self-harms, it feels as if it will offer the emotional relief they need.

WHAT'S BEHIND THE REASONS PEOPLE INFLICT INJURY?

Behavior experts tell us there are many driving factors behind why people self-harm. Let's examine the major reasons.

Reason 1: To Feel Better/Physically, Express Emotional Pain

When I returned home from Afghanistan, my family soon discovered I wasn't the same man who left nine months earlier to serve overseas. The inner turmoil I felt because of the death and destruction I witnessed wore heavily on my conscience.

One evening some four months later, I kicked in the door to my girlfriend's house and began threatening the people inside. Most evenings I self-medicated with alcohol to numb my feelings, and this was another one of those nights. I didn't know how to express the emotional anguish I was in without feeling judged or having people think I was crazy. Instead, I lashed out in fits of anger or violent paranoia. Everything I was doing was a physical manifestation of the pain I felt internally.

In my story, it's easy for you to spot why I acted out. My emotional pain was driving the destructive habits in my life. However, when talking about self-harm, the question posed is, "Why would someone hurt themselves? How can that possibly help what they're going through?"

The reality is that people often self-harm as an external manifestation of the internal pain or emotions they're going through in the same way that I did with alcohol. The internal emotions they feel can be a result of numerous reasons: trauma, abuse, bullying, not living up to their own standards, depression, stress, family issues, and the list goes on. The triggers can be minor or major crises.

One woman within our community at HeartSupport explained, "It's like getting on a roller coaster. The tension and emotional pain you feel slowly builds the same way a roller coaster starts its slow climb before it reaches the summit, then begins its wild descent. When you finally cut, the rush kicks in."

Yale psychologist Mitchell J. Prinstein, a researcher on self-harm, states, "By far the most common reason people said they self-injured was to stop feeling so bad."

By injuring themselves, many users report feeling emotional relief when they hurt themselves as a way to push down intense emotions (like anger or anxiety) that can often feel too overwhelming. The result is that their self-punishment (which we'll explore shortly) helps distract them from their other emotions, thus teaching them a new, yet harmful method to cope. The idea that people were writing their emotions onto their body is the very reason why we named this book "ReWrite."

Whatever the cause, self-harming, to that person, feels like the safest way to communicate that pain. For me, I was afraid of being judged and seen as a monster if people heard what I went through and experienced overseas. Similarly, people who self-harm can be afraid of that same kind of judgment and rejection if they choose to reveal their emotional wounds. Because of this, it feels as if the only option (or the only option that makes sense), is to self-harm, because it's the safest way to communicate that pain.

Reason 2: As a Method of Control

If you're like most people, you've probably tried to control a few things in your life.

Anything from your financial situation to the way a crush might feel about you. Maybe you've even done something to directly influence the outcome.

Many people we've encountered over the years explain that they use self-injury as a way to establish control in their lives. Say, for instance, you're a teenager being bullied at the local high school. Each day you're shoved into lockers, made fun of, tripped, or belittled. You report the events, but it only makes the situation worse. Not only can you not control the way people feel about you or respond, there seems to be little anyone else can do either.

In short, you feel powerless about your situation. It doesn't just feel like you're drowning; it feels like you're being held there and like there's nothing you can do to surface for air. Even though the choice to self-harm causes pain, it's a pain you get to choose. Instead of being the recipient of pain, you get to be the decider. That autonomy, choice, and control in the midst of powerlessness feels like a breath and a reminder that, "I am still a human, and I still have a say in my life."

Reason 3: To Feel Something Other Than Numbness

In the movie *Fight Club*, to escape insomnia and a boring, unfulfilled life, Edward Norton's character ends up inventing an alter-ego (played by Brad Pitt). This dissociation eventually leads to recruiting other members to their underground fight club and causing genuine anarchy throughout the city. Many men beg to join the club to escape the monotony of day-to-day life and proceed to fight one another until bloody and broken.

If art imitates life, then in this example, we see how in order to escape the numbness and deadness they feel in their lives, the characters inflict pain on one another, which morphs into a camaraderie.

Many who self-harm use it as a method to feel something other than the numbness or deadness they feel inside. Inflicting pain is a simple way for them to feel something once more. The reasons behind this can ultimately vary. The numbness can stem from depression, years of abuse (emotional and physical), rape or sexual assault, or a chemical imbalance.

In some cases the person with past trauma will, just like Edward Norton's character in *Fight Club*, dissociate from a past event that is too difficult to face. The result is an inner numbness, and by cutting or harming themselves, they begin to feel something once more.

Reason 4: To Self-Punish

Kasey was a cheerleader at her local high school and a straight-A student. On the surface she was well liked, popular, and seemed to have a good family life. Whereas other girls on the squad dealt with eating disorders, Kasey would cut herself on areas her clothes covered. When she ate too many calories, she cut. When she performed less than stellar on an exam, she cut. When she had drama with friends, she cut. When she looked in the mirror and didn't see the perfect body, she cut.

Growing up, she often felt a high amount of pressure from her parents to succeed. When she didn't live up to those standards, she saw the disappointment she caused them, and she hated feeling as if she was to blame for their pain. It seemed that when they punished her, things got better.

As her life went on, she began to believe that to right her wrongs, she had to punish herself for the pain she caused others or where she failed to live up to her own standards. She would tell herself, "You're dumb, you're worthless, you're a failure, you're fat, and you deserve this."

In essence, self-harming allowed her to even the score; the pain she inflicted on others and her missteps caused her to injure herself as penance. By doing this in private, she could exact justice on herself without ever having to confront the people she'd let down or feel the pain of their disappointment. She felt better when she cut because self-harm became her blame-eraser, and she'd paid her dues for her own failures.

Many parents don't realize the emotional weight of the expectations and pressure they put on their children. Combined with the pressures of today's social media culture where you have to present your life perfectly online, many teenagers, twenty-somethings, and adults feel they are living below the expectations others have for them.

This heavy emotional burden—one that often negatively affects performance, happiness, and self-worth—can carry over to their job performance later in life, and something they do as a result of believing they "deserve it." However, their reason to self-punish can also be a result of abuse, sexual trauma, or post-traumatic stress. We'll explore this more in chapter 4.

Reason 5: To Distract Attention from Trauma

In chapter 1, I relayed the story of Leanna who cut herself because of the trauma she faced as a victim of child sex trafficking. Others are victims of sexual assault. They are young men and women who've been abused by their parents, a teacher, or a relative. Still others may have post-traumatic stress disorder. No matter the reason, this victimization often explains why some people self-injure.

In the TV show *The Magicians*, a priest helps lead rehab and 12-Step for addicts. Later in the show, you discover that he left his son in a hot car for hours while grabbing booze. His son's death propelled him further into alcoholism. The alcohol distracted him from having to deal with the guilt of his son's death and numbed his feelings.

Those who self-injure can have a similar mentality where instead of facing past events that can be emotional torture for them, they shift their focus to the pain they inflict on themselves in order to avoid thinking about the event or the shame and guilt they harbor.

WHAT ABOUT THE PSYCHOLOGY AND SCIENCE BEHIND SELF-HARM?

A big reason why self-harm becomes extremely addicting and difficult to break free from is that it works as both a positive and negative reinforcement.

If you've ever had a dog, you understand positive reinforcement. In order to teach Fido to sit, lie down, or roll over, many people will use a doggie treat to reinforce positive behavior. As a child your parents will warn you of the dangers of a hot stove, yet many children will touch it anyway. When they are burned, they learn never to touch a hot stove again. This is an example of negative reinforcement.

Self-injury offers both positive and negative reinforcement neurologically, both by altering emotions and by altering relationships with other people. For instance, the person who uses self-harm to return from numbness (reason 3) is an example of positive reinforcement by altering their emotions. The pain sends the signal that "if I cut, now I can feel."

Others, however, may use self-harm to punish themselves and thereby use negative reinforcement. Still others could injure themselves to demonstrate their emotional pain in order to get a loved one to react (positive reinforcement) or to stop doing something (negative reinforcement). Thus a person's reasons for self-injury can be different each time, effectively training the brain to respond to both.

What this effectively does is rewire a person's brain, so the behavior itself becomes highly addictive. Neuroscience is discovering among those who self-injure (as well as other behaviors) that such habits begin to shape and rewire neurological pathways to become more than just a behavioral choice.

An article on the website of the American Psychological Association, for example, reports that what these techniques do is create pain offset by relief conditioning. Scientists found that if you paired pain with a stimulus, over time, people would react more favorably to the pain because they had learned to associate it with pain relief. For instance, when researchers shocked rats and then presented them with a pleasant odor, over time, the rats began seeking out the smell.

In regard to the psychological aspect, researcher Jill Hooley and her team from Harvard found that those who self-injure developed a negative self-image as well. When asked to describe themselves, self-injurers responded with words such as *bad, defective,* or *deserving of punishment.* Upon reviewing this research, another researcher of nonsuicidal self-injury, Joseph Franklin, studied why people would undertake this behavior. According to the same article from the American Psychological Association, "He [Franklin] looked at it in context of the fact that most people probably like themselves and therefore don't want to hurt themselves. In ongoing, still unpublished work, Franklin asked participants to rate words like "me," "myself" and "I" on a 10-point scale ranging from most unpleasant to most pleasant. Most people rated themselves between a seven and eight, but self-injurers gave themselves only a two or a three."

As you can see, because of the psychological and neurological conditioning self-harm offers, the practice quickly becomes habit, and thus requires help and new strategies to break the destructive tendencies. Fortunately the brain is resilient and can repair itself with time.

In the next chapter I'll directly address the key factors behind why many people, not just self-injurers, have a negative self-image: guilt and shame.

To watch the accompanying videos that recap the chapter and provide a case study, visit http:// heartsupport.com/SH

4

DEALING WITH GUILT AND SHAME

I had to dive deep and think about what caused the behaviors. A lot of times it can feel like you're in a cycle of shame/guilt/numbness that leads to self-harm, which in turn leads to more self-harm. I found it was important to look at what was causing the shame, the guilt, and the numbness besides the self-harm. It takes a lot of searching yourself, which, at times, can be painful and feel terrible. —Nikki

Most people don't understand the difference between guilt and shame. They assume these feelings are just different sides of the same coin.

Imagine, however, the following scenario. Jason grows up in a normal home, goes to college on a scholarship, but one evening has too much to drink with his friends and drives drunk. He smashes his car into a tree and is arrested by police and charged with driving while intoxicated. He will obviously experience feelings of guilt because he broke the law and had the potential to have seriously injured himself or killed someone else in an auto accident. In his mind he may think, "I really screwed up."

Let's say, though, that after his hearing and trial his girlfriend tells him what a loser he is for driving drunk, and his parents bring it up every time he goes home, reminding him just how much he screwed up. Inevitably, he starts to have the thought, "I'm a terrible human being. How could I have done that? I'm worthless."

In this example, Jason initially has feelings of guilt because of a mistake he made. Guilt says, "I did something bad." However, when his girlfriend and parents began to remind him over and over of his failure, he begins to operate in a shame mentality. Shame effectively tells us, "I *am* bad."

Guilt, then, is feeling bad about what we did, and shame is feeling bad about who we are. Shame is a parasite in our recovery; the more shame we have, the harder our recovery gets because if we believe we *are* bad, then we have a harder time believing that we deserve to get better.

Unfortunately, many in our society believe shame is a tool to shape up someone's behavior. Take, for instance, a boss who tells his employee, "If you really cared about this company and your job, you'd work harder." The message that's sent is not that the employee made a mistake that can be corrected, but instead a shame message that says, "You're lazy, and you're a bad employee."

The boss believes these messages will motivate the employee to do a better job to avoid the pain of feeling like a bad employee. But it erodes a person's confidence that they have what it takes to actually do a better job, and it can keep them stuck in a cycle of underperformance.

Researcher Brené Brown confirms this observation after interviewing thousands of people around the topics of shame and vulnerability over the course of a decade:

> We live in a world where most people still subscribe to the belief that shame is a good tool for keeping people in line. Not only is this wrong, but it's dangerous. Shame is highly correlated with addiction, violence, aggression, depression, eating disorders, and bullying. Researchers don't find shame correlated with positive outcomes at all—there are no data to support that shame is a helpful compass for good behavior. In fact, shame is much more likely to be the cause of destructive and hurtful behaviors than it is to be the solution.

Many caring friends and parents often unintentionally use shame to try to motivate their loved ones in their recovery as well. It can sound something like this: "If you really wanted to and you cared about how much it hurts me, you'd stop the self-harm."

While this is a common response, it effectively says, "If you really cared about me, you'd stop, but you don't, and that makes you a bad person because you don't care about *how it makes me feel.*" People use self-harm as a relief for emotional pain, so causing them to feel worse about themselves often won't motivate them to use less; it will give them reason to want to do it more.

Note for family and friends: Shame statements are unhelpful because they make the self-harm about someone else's pain (yours). When someone who self-harms chooses to open up to you—a parent or friend—even though they're deathly afraid of being judged, it's vital for their vulnerability to be met with your understanding and empathy.

If instead they're met with a message that makes them feel ashamed for what they're struggling with and earnestly searching for help to overcome, your feelings will become a roadblock to your relationship with them and their recovery. It's imperative that you process your own emotions so you can be available to help them with theirs. You'll find space in the workbook to begin that process, and you'll learn how to respond in a more helpful way in the concluding chapter written for friends and family.

Meanwhile, the only solution to overcoming the shame you have about your self-injury is by talking about it. That's because shame works by keeping you alone. You start to believe, "If they know who I really am, they'll never love me." You fear opening up to others because you fear they'll confirm the shame you feel toward yourself. So you isolate, which feels logical, spend time with fewer people, experience less judgment, feel less shame. But shame festers in isolation. Being alone is not only a trigger for some, it keeps you from connecting with others, which is an essential step toward healing.

In a similar way, shame promises protection, but it causes you pain. Shame says: "If I believe these negative things about myself, I won't be taken by surprise when other people tell me I'm worthless too." It feels as if it's preventing you from future pain by being prepared for the worst others could say or think about you.

But in reality, shame doesn't defend you from the pain from others, it turns you into your own worst enemy. You have more opportunities than everyone else combined to tell yourself, "I am worthless." So even if it did lessen the pain from others, the trade-off wouldn't be worth it.

Sadly, the worst part is that shame actually doesn't help you feel less bad when people shame you; it confirms the worthlessness you feel and spirals you into more misery. And when you're miserable, you've learned to use self-harm as a relief.

The less we talk about shame, the more and more control it has over our lives. But that doesn't mean it's easy to talk about. Part of the reason we feel so much tension, resistance, and fear around shame has to do with it being vitally important toward our healing and growth. If we didn't have those feelings, then it wouldn't matter that much to us would it?

For instance, let's say you're musically gifted and have an incredible voice. However, you're terrified of singing in public or at a concert. The thought of actually having to sing in front of a crowd causes a ball of tension in your gut when you think about it. Despite your closest friends and family members encouraging you, there's a deep resistance you feel toward actually acting on their advice.

Internally, the message you may be hearing is, "What if people laugh at me? What if I'm rejected? What if my voice cracks? People will think I'm pathetic, and it will only prove that I am. It's better to play it safe and not risk public embarrassment."

Resistance is most often associated with shame messages we tell ourselves that keep us from connecting, growing, or healing. Yet, the more resistance we feel, the more certain we can be that it's something we *have* to do. Resistance is like a compass that always points true north. If we follow it north, it will force us to confront our shame. This is why sharing our story and struggle with someone is so vital. (Ideally that person would be emotionally healthy and prone to respond with empathy and compassion.)

How do you go about doing this, you may be asking? By taking bold and courageous steps when you're terrified to the core about what others may think of your battle with self-injury, let alone the shame you may be feeling every waking hour.

FIGHTING SHAME AND DEVELOPING A RESILIENT SPIRIT

Author Brené Brown shares four key methods in her book *Daring Greatly* that I've modified to help lead you toward empathy and healing. You can begin using these steps to fight shame and develop the grit needed to bounce back. We'll also explore these concepts more in our workbook section.

1. **Recognizing the Shame You Feel from Self-Harm and When You're Triggered by It.** When you feel shame about self-harm, can you recognize it? Can you wade through what feelings are connected to it and the environment or event that triggered it?

2. **Connection and Community.** Are you connecting with others and sharing your story with trusted friends? If not, you have no one to encourage you in this journey.

3. **Authentic Conversations about How You Feel.** Are you talking openly about what you need when you're struggling and how people can best support you?

4. **Practicing Critical Awareness, Reflection, and Gratitude.** Remember shame messages are often false. Can you sort through what's true and what's not in your emotions? As you reflect on your week (working in the workbook), it will be important to celebrate your small victories to develop a resilient spirit.

These methods, though heavily modified, are what can become a "strategy for protecting connection" and developing shame resilience—the ability to understand when false messages are attacking you. The goal is to begin to combat the shame you feel from self-harm and eventually stand on your own against these false narratives.

It is important to note that you may feel guilt for self-injuring—and to some level that needs to be there as an indicator that something needs to change. Remember that guilt reminds us that we did something bad, not that we are bad. There may be remorse in your life for scars acquired due to self-injury. You can view this remorse in two ways: The shame message would be something like this: "I'm worthless, I deserve these scars, and it's proof I can't change." Guilt, however, may look more like this: "If this continues unchecked, I'll only stay stuck. I wish I could change. I want to change."

Without a desire to change, we don't have the ability to take proactive steps to heal. The hard reality is that as much as we may say we want things to change, until we actually begin to take even a baby step, nothing in our lives will change. We will only have ourselves to blame for remaining where we are.

Like Nikki pointed out in the introduction to this chapter, when you begin to confront the underlying shame and guilt, it will be hard and may even feel terribly painful. Perhaps it's best to think of it like this then:

Suppose you have broken your leg, but never had it cast and continue to walk on it until it becomes unbearable. One day you arrive at the doctor's office. He tells you that unfortunately the leg has healed incorrectly, which is why it's so painful. He explains that in order for it to heal, he's going to have to break the leg and reset it so that it can heal correctly.

The initial break hurt obviously, but when the doctor sets your leg, the after-effects may hurt as well. The same holds true when confronting the shame, guilt, numbness, trauma, or pain associated with self-injury. It's going to hurt initially.

If we are to heal, we must face the dragon in the caves of our hearts that's clawing about. It may seem overwhelming. It may seem impossible. But just remember, the more you feel that resistance and tension, the more you can be sure it's the path toward your recovery.

To watch the accompanying videos that recap the chapter and provide a case study, visit http:// heartsupport.com/SH

5

RECOVERY

(Let Me Tell You about Willpower...
and Why It Doesn't Work)

The most pivotal moment for me was being 100 percent honest about my self-harm and struggles, and then receiving acceptance. There's so much shame and misunderstanding associated with self-harm, and the biggest way that I was helped was just by people loving me unconditionally. —Kayla

WILLPOWER DOESN'T WORK

Most of the staff at HeartSupport has been through 12-Step for various reasons. Jake, the founder of HeartSupport and lead singer of August Burns Red, found himself recovering from wounds he didn't even know existed from his childhood. He had buried them for many years, only to discover they would later affect his adult life.

During his 12-Step process, he went through a painful divorce that fueled a message he heard internally throughout most of his life: "Everyone is eventually going to abandon you."

Jake spent most of his life believing that narrative, and here's what he tried to do for years to combat it: simply use willpower to not believe it.

He discovered willpower alone only led to further destructive patterns because he kept failing and even returning him to old habits of binge drinking. When he began working The Steps, he discovered that Step One was this: We admitted we were powerless over our addiction—that our lives had become unmanageable.

His sponsor explained that as a former alcoholic, "Most alcoholics, for reasons yet unknown, have lost the power of choice in drink. Our so-called willpower becomes practically nonexistent." So Jake's first step was admitting he had a problem with abandonment and then admitting he was powerless to change himself.

At this point, you've probably discovered willpower doesn't work in regard to quitting self-mutilation behavior. We're quite sure you've tried over and over again, made promises, pinky swore, and yet there's little to no change. If quitting was as simple as white-knuckling your will, then we wouldn't have addicts of any sort would we?

The most important mental shift you can admit coming into the recovery process is realizing that your willpower alone won't fix this issue. It's like being a carpenter who's trying to build a table, but the only tool in your arsenal is a ruler. You may have the measurements for how to accomplish it, but you're completely lacking in the tools to build the table. You can't delude yourself into thinking that you can create a masterpiece. The only way you can build the table is by admitting you don't have the tools and then beginning to gather them to start work.

That's exactly what we'll be doing in the chapter.

YOU HAVE TO WANT TO CHANGE

For me, I got so tired of what I was doing to myself and thought, "This is it. This has to change." — Jeremy

One of the reasons people enter the 12-Step program is because they realize things have gotten out of hand, and they want to change. You cannot help people who don't want to change. In the TV show *Intervention*, they coach families with the following advice: "There is nothing we won't do to help you get better. But there is nothing more we will do to help this continue anymore."

By drawing a line in the sand, the family discovers whether or not their loved one is serious about change, or if they would rather continue in their habits and addiction.

> **Note for family and friends:** If you're a family member reading this, be sure you've read the chapter on how to help, because if you only take a hard stance, things will go horribly wrong.

Choice is a powerful motivator for the first step in recovery. Imagine you decide you want to run a marathon this year. When you choose to do it, it's a first step toward commitment. From there, you either put an action plan in place to train for the marathon, or you simply dream about doing it.

Some people may not be ready to make this mental shift. You may even be asking yourself, "How do I know if I'm ready to make a change or not?"

You're ready to change if—

- You feel as if your self-harm controls you more than you control it.
- You want to be able to imagine a life without self-harm.
- You believe you deserve to be free from self-harm.
- You are open to listen to and follow the advice from others to help you recover.
- You are willing to make deliberate and even difficult changes in your life to aid your recovery.
- You are more committed to making a way than you are to making excuses.
- You are willing to stick with it until you succeed.
- You are doing this for yourself.

You're not ready to change if—

- You feel as if you're mostly in control of your self-harm problem.
- You're willing to make changes as long as they

don't require you to do anything drastic.
- You're expecting that reading (not applying) this book is supposed to be your cure.
- You don't believe you deserve to be free from self-harm.
- You're okay if you try this and don't end up getting better.
- You don't want to imagine your life without self-harm.
- You are doing this for someone else other than yourself or because you have to.

If you want to be ready to change but aren't there yet, you can find questions in the workbook that will help you process and overcome that hurdle.

If you're choosing to move forward to begin the healing process from self-harm, then what we'll be doing from here on out is outlining next steps and tips. Later, you'll see daily activities, exercises, and prompts you'll need to complete to continue on your path toward healing.

Just wanting to change is a start, but there's more to it. You may find yourself in situations that continue to be triggering or in destructive environments, and willpower alone won't fix this struggle.

ENVIRONMENT VS. WILLPOWER

There are people willing to listen to you. Even if you think that there's not, I promise there is. People who love and care about you, or third-party resources that genuinely want the best for

you. One law I live by now is surrounding myself with greatness, people who think beautiful deep thoughts, are motivated, and want to be a positive change in this world. People who have goals and will stop at nothing to get them. A change like this is no easy task, as it involves a lot of self-awareness, and it may require you to cut some deep ties. But a change like this could change your life.
—Charles

In January each year, people make New Year's resolutions. Going to the gym is top among these resolutions, but 80 percent of people fail before the month is even up. What gives?

Most people are stuck in the exact same environment they were in in December once January rolls around. They're in their office, back at school, eating at their favorite restaurant, or drinking their favorite wine. Imagine you're a college student who wants to be healthy and exercise, but all your friends keep eating fast food and convincing you to go to happy hour on Wednesday. Your resolve is going to crumble quickly.

Now think about your current environment. Where are you when you want to engage in self-harm? What events are happening? Are there people in your life that fuel the desire to harm yourself? Are you alone when you self-harm? What environments are particularly triggering?

One of the most important realizations you can have in regard to combating self-harm is that your environment is more powerful than your willpower. As human beings, we are more often than not the product of the environments we surround ourselves with.

Here's an example. Jane is a college student who lives by herself in a dorm room. Because of the pressure of making good grades and her family's expectations to succeed, she finds herself cutting as a source of control.

By examining Jane's hypothetical situation, we can uncover a few things about her environment.

- She lives alone so she probably is alone when she cuts.
- The college environment she lives in is less about getting an education, but more the pressure to succeed.
- Her family's expectations feed her disruptive environment as well.

Now, imagine Jane tries to quit self-injury through will-power alone, but her environment stays the same. What are her chances of recovery? Probably not that good.

She's certainly not doomed to failure, but changing your environment can be some of the easiest decisions that make the most impact to your recovery. Willpower is dependent on saying no when you really want to say yes. And recovery certainly requires willpower. But our environment makes it easier for us because it decreases the number of times we have to say no.

For instance, if loneliness is a trigger for Jane, she has to say no more often living alone than if she lived with multiple roommates who were dependably there. Making this environmental change could help alleviate some of the pressure she feels to self-harm. In turn, it could help build her confidence early on in her recovery, develop momentum, and help her use her willpower for other moments that environmental changes wouldn't be able to help.

Because environment can be one of the most powerful tools to aid recovery, let's look at a few environments that may be fueling the desire to self-injure that may need to change:

- Are you alone when you injure? If so, you may need to find a roommate or not allow yourself to be alone. When the desire strikes, you may have to visit public places to ensure your recovery process.

- Are you in a high-pressure job or schooling environment? The strong desire to injure may come from failed expectations in an environment that only heaps more and more pressure on. In order to recover, sometimes drastic steps have to be taken, and finding a new job or school might be the next step.

- Do the people you hang out with have addictions or self-injure also? Are they unhealthy relationally? "You are the company you keep." We'll cover this more in the Community section later in this chapter, but being around people who fuel your addiction is only going to keep you stuck in it.

- Are you bored with life and feel you're not meeting your goals or are purposeless? Many times when we're bored or feel stuck in a rut, it's self-imposed. If life feels like a black hole, then perhaps there aren't enough things filling it. We'll explore this concept more in the Service section.

- Are you in an unhealthy romantic relationship? For some a toxic relationship can be the source of their self-harm, but fear of loneliness keeps them in the cycle.

These are just a few examples of environments that may explain why recovery seems completely impossible. When you get to the journal section of this book, you will discover sections meant to walk you through your environments and questions to hold you accountable.

At this point you may be feeling some form of resistance to all of this. Fear even. Changing an environment you've known for so long and facing uncertainty or loss of a friend group or a toxic job may sound like too much. But the resistance you're feeling, above all things, is a liar.

Author Steven Pressfield has perhaps the best explanation as to why we experience so much resistance around the areas in our lives where things need to change or have to. He said, "Resistance is experienced as fear; the degree of fear equates to the strength of Resistance. Therefore the more fear we feel about a specific enterprise, the more certain we can be that that enterprise is important to us and to the growth of our soul. That's why we feel so much Resistance. If it meant nothing to us, there'd be no Resistance."

For centuries sailors used Polaris (the North Star) as

their "true north." Anytime they got off course, they could look to the night sky and course correct. Resistance does the same thing. It always points you in the direction you should be heading. The reason that fear and gut check tends to happen is because deep down we know it's what we should do.

Sadly, most times we listen to the voice of resistance and continue to stay stuck in the environments that are killing us. What's the voice of resistance telling you? Why is it a liar? We'll explore these questions and more in the journaling section to promote growth. But perhaps the biggest voice of resistance is the one telling you to keep quiet and tell no one. To become exposed would mean a step toward vulnerability, and often becoming vulnerable is something we all have resistance to.

VULNERABILITY

What's the bravest thing you've seen someone do in public or among your friends? Was it a time when they shared something open and honestly that could have been perceived as weak?

A few years ago, Jake, the founder of HeartSupport who was mentioned earlier, came to the team and informed us he wasn't fit to lead the organization. Jake was smack-dab in the middle of recovery, a divorce, and had relapsed and was drinking to numb his depression. The team stepped in to continue running the organization while Jake continued recovery. The process was messy and full of victories and relapse. A year later, Jake had found healing and was ready to step into the arena once more.

Over a phone conversation late one evening, a team member encouraged Jake to be vulnerable with the community at HeartSupport and his fans. At HeartSupport we believe in the power of story and vulnerability. A common myth is that vulnerability is weakness, but we're willing to bet that some of the people you think are most courageous have shared very vulnerable things openly. When you allow yourself to be vulnerable in front of others, it gives them the courage and opportunity to do the same.

During the call, our team member ended up telling Jake this simple truth: "You cannot demand vulnerability of the community and your fans without doing it yourself. That's the paradox of vulnerability. The last thing you want others to see in you is vulnerability and your hurts, but it's the first thing you look for in others."

Realizing he wanted to be honest and take courageous steps, Jake ended up sharing with our entire community and internet about how he had relapsed and had struggled through deep depression and made some poor choices. He even left all the ugly details in. How do you think people responded?

People were amazed at his transparency and shared how they thought it was brave for him to share hard secrets he had kept from people. It gave numerous others the chance to share their hurts as well with him and the team at HeartSupport because he chose to open up first.

But What If I Get Rejected?

That's the scary thing about vulnerability. The ability to face betrayal. While vulnerability means emotional exposure is evident along with the possibility of getting wounded, it doesn't mean you just go tell the world on social media about your struggle with self-harm. Vulnerability requires trust.

When my wife, Emily, was in high school, she found out her group of friends had been spreading rumors. Another girl in the group claimed Emily had been flirting with her boyfriend. When she confronted the lie, the rest of the girls abandoned her.

The betrayal by her closest friends and the shock accompanying it pulled her into a deep depression for many years. It would not be until college that she found people she could be vulnerable with and believe they wouldn't spread rumors about her.

What Emily learned was that trust operated like a glass of water. There were people who would refill her water glass, and those who would sip and steal from it. The people who proved over time that they were givers as opposed to takers, she came to trust and could be vulnerable in front of. They were the ones she could rely on and were a constant source of stability, as opposed to friends we may have whose lives carry more drama than security.

Sometimes those who refill our proverbial glass will be a close friend or a parent. Other times a pastor or counselor. The point of Emily's story is that trust is built one deposit at a time and should be the same when choosing those we confide in about our struggle with self-injury.

So how do you begin the small steps toward vulnerability? It begins by owning your story.

THE POWER OF YOUR STORY

Consider the story line from the epic fantasy novel and movie *Lord of the Rings* for a moment. A young Hobbit named Frodo Baggins discovers a ring of power built to enslave mankind by the dark lord, Sauron. He embarks on a journey along with humans, elves, dwarves, and a magician to destroy it and battle the forces of darkness. Along the way he succumbs more and more to the evil power of the ring—and that's where the story ends! If you know the books or movie, you know this is hardly the case, but imagine if that were the story's ending?

In the same respect, your story is still being written, and when you own your story and recognize the power behind it, you'll see you have the opportunity to face the conflict and hurt you're currently facing. It's important to remember that just like a story has chapters, our own lives have chapters as well.

One of the reasons we're compelled to keep watching movies and reading books is because the stakes are high. Just when the hero is about to win, tragedy or failure strikes. We, as the viewer, are then forced to know how it's all going to work out. The tension, failure, and struggle all keep us turning pages. Without these chapters, we could not be convinced of an epic ending or moments of victory because, let's be honest, that's not how real life works.

Right now, this chapter of your life may seem dark and hopeless, but can be part of a bigger story that's not over yet. Self-harm may pop up in chapters but does not have to be the main theme in your greater story. But this all begins by owning the chapter of the story you're in now.

At HeartSupport, we've watched people share their stories on our support wall with others and let their vulnerability and struggle show. When they own their story, they get to write a new ending because they begin to realize they have a community rooting for the hero (them) to slay the beast (their struggle).

When we push down hurt or pretend that our struggle with self-harm doesn't exist, it will own us and move us back into cycles of shame, isolation, and emotional pain. We may say we have a good story in the midst of one that is dark and stormy, but we'd only be deluding ourselves. Instead, own your story. Engage the feelings behind it. Perhaps more importantly, what are the false narratives in your story that aren't true? Each of us makes up stories in our minds that aren't true.

For instance, imagine you're at work and your boss is short with you because of a big deadline everyone is trying to meet. You normally have a great relationship with your boss, and she often praises you for your hard work and dedication. However, because of her reaction you feel that she views you as incapable and that you're just a drain on the workplace. These feelings make you want to injure yourself.

What's true in this story and what's not? It's true that your boss was curt and everyone is hustling to meet a deadline. What's not true is that your boss views you as a drain and incapable. That's a story you made up.

Owning your story means engaging your feelings and seeking out what's true and what's not. A story driven by emotion and self-protection probably doesn't involve accuracy, logic, or the truth. There's a good chance you're not being honest with yourself if your story is only driven by raw emotion.

So what's the story you're telling yourself? This will be an important question once we get to the workbook section and that you'll explore more. However, simply throwing out your story may make you feel better, but in order for changes to begin, we need people to help us along the path. Don't worry, we'll cover this process more in the workbook section.

INSTILL SEVERAL FORMS OF FEEDBACK/ ACCOUNTABILITY

Going back to the *Lord of the Rings* example, even though Frodo eventually succumbed to the power of the ring, he had several forms of accountability and people giving him feedback as far as how to proceed. His closest and best friend Samwise was the anchor he could rely on when he was too weak to carry on. Gandalf the wizard provided wisdom and discernment. Merry and Pippin created adventure and laughter, while Aragorn helped defend Frodo in dire situations.

In 12-Step and recovery communities you'll often hear about someone having a "sponsor." This is someone who's also gone through recovery and is there to support and counsel. A sponsor doesn't even have to have been through the same addiction or struggle. They are there to help you process and give feedback, and are in a more emotionally healthy spot. So think of them more as mentors than sponsors.

If you can imagine the plot of *Stars Wars*, these mentors would be the "Yodas" in your life. Mentors are those who can speak into the areas of your life and provide clarity to the areas you're struggling in. By having someone you can call or check in with whom you trust and who provides empathy and clarity while holding you to a high standard, you'll begin to take proactive steps in the right direction.

The person or people you select should be in a stable spot and who you trust. This could be a friend, counselor, pastor, coach, spouse, or parent. Like Frodo's companions, a mentor can provide different emotional aspects you may find helpful in your recovery. The more community you build, the better, and will be vital in perhaps the most important aspect of your recovery: community.

COMMUNITY

Johann Hari is a journalist who began researching the war on drugs only to discover something immensely fascinating. His discoveries led to a well-known TED talk entitled "Everything you think you know about addiction is wrong."

In the talk, he meets a professor of psychology in Vancouver, Canada, named Bruce Alexander. Professor Alexander found that the way we view addiction comes partly from a series of experiments that were done in the twentieth century.

Scientists put rats in a cage and gave them two water bottles to choose from. One bottle contained normal water. The other was laced with either heroin or cocaine. The rats would always choose the water with drugs in it and would almost always kill themselves quickly. Most of these reports are where we point to in order to show the addictive nature of drugs.

Professor Alexander, however, noticed something. The rats were always alone in a cage, so they had little else to do except consume drugs. With that in mind, he set out to create another experiment using the same principles. This time he created what he called "Rat Park." The park was a giant cage with tunnels to explore, tons of other rats, lots of cheese, and colored balls. To replicate the experiment, he gave the rats two water bottles like the original experiment: drugged water and regular water.

Here's the fascinating part. In Rat Park, rats don't like the drug water and almost never use it. None of the rats ever use it compulsively or overdose. Hari goes on to draw similar comparisons to the country of Portugal where they decriminalized all drugs and instead spend the money they used to combat drugs to reconnect addicts with society. In the past fifteen years, drug use went down 50 percent! Hari concludes his talk posing the question that what if the way we cope, numb out, or get addicted has more to do with a lack of community, and more with isolation than anything else?

At HeartSupport, one thing we've seen over and over is the power of community. People have gone from alone and addicted to connected and thriving. What changed?

Each person we've seen overcome monumental self-harm or addictive struggles went from a place of isolation to discovering a community that cares about them.

Julie, for example, is a young woman we met while on Vans Warped Tour one year who was stuck in cycles of self-harm and self-hate. She had given up on life and planned to commit suicide. However, utilizing the power of our online community, finding accountability, and serving with other volunteers, she's now been clean for over three years. She volunteers every summer in the HeartSupport tent on Vans Warped Tour sharing her story of hope with others struggling.

What advice does she have for others? Surround yourself with a community that believes and can encourage you even when you fall down.

SERVICE

> I slept and dreamt that life was joy. I awoke and saw that life was service. I acted and behold, service was joy. —Rabindranath Tagore

Stephan is a young man we met when HeartSupport first began who chronically self-injured (you learned about him in the Introduction). Like Julie, he was disconnected and alone. His life slowly began to change when he got connected with HeartSupport and later with a community at his local church. However, some of the monumental growth came when he began serving others.

Many of those who self-injure tell us stories. They feel little to no direction and purpose in life. As we explained in earlier chapters, they injure to return from the deadness and monotony of life or as an escape. One of the most powerful impacts we've seen among men and women struggling is to begin volunteering or serving somewhere. As most of their time was spent isolated and led to injury, serving somewhere allowed them to interact in public places with other people who were passionate about the things they were.

Additionally, if you lack a community, serving somewhere is the fastest way to find a community with similar interests. Do you love animals? Serve at an animal shelter. Do you want to help end homelessness? Serve at a shelter or soup kitchen. Do you love music and concerts? There are plenty of festivals each year looking for passionate volunteers.

The more time you spend serving others, the less time you'll have to injure and the more you'll be thinking of the needs of others instead of your own. One of our volunteers once told us how he had begun to help mentor teenagers. He realized that by serving he had to be a positive role model in the lives of impressionable kids. This caused him to begin making progressive changes in his life that helped lead him toward healing and wholeness.

In our exercises later in the book, we'll have suggestions of things you can do to serve.

ADDITIONAL ACCOUNTABILITY/HELP

Distraction Can Become Passion

Have you ever wanted to learn another language? Write music? Learn to play the guitar? Write poetry or a novel? Maybe even learn a new skill?

One of the key things you can do when you feel the urge to injure is to use your time and energy proactively to do something you're passionate about. The key to recovery is all about pause. When the moment comes that you feel the desire to harm yourself, it's an opportunity to do something else instead. As we discussed earlier, a change in environment can be the key thing to keep you from injuring yourself.

For instance, let's say you've always wanted to learn how to write and blog, but you have no idea how to. While at home one day and after a disappointing day at work, you have the urge to self-harm. Instead, you immediately hop in the car, drive to a coffee shop, and begin researching your passion—learning how to write.

Because of the numerous online courses and sites offering advice and skills, this is a passion project you can spend hours and years working. Each time, you feel the urge, you do the same thing. After some time you begin writing and honing the craft more and more. Slowly over time, your mind will begin to associate that urge and replace it with an urge to write, thus doing something productive, but also beneficial to your personal growth, and who knows where it could lead from there (a large blog following, a novel you've written, or even a job in journalism).

By taking the urge and changing your environment through a positive distraction, you can help cultivate your passions and keep yourself free from potentially harming yourself.

Here are just a few examples of activities that may give you ideas. In our exercise portion, we'll have weekly ideas for you to consider.

Distraction Ideas (YouTube and the Internet Will Be Your Best Friend)

- Make a website, create an app, or just learn to code.
- Learn to sing or take vocal lessons and practice.
- Learn how to repair something.
- Begin writing poetry and studying how to construct it.
- Pick up an artistic skill like illustration, painting, or photography.
- Learn martial arts or self-defense.
- Learn how to design things stylistically (for example, fashion design, interior design).
- Learn how to build electronic hardware.
- Learn a new instrument or how to play one.
- Become a cooking pro and create elaborate dishes for your friends and family.
- Learn a new language (Duolingo is a free app).
- Become a writer or a blogger and practice writing daily.

Recovery Communities/12-Step

A common misconception that runs throughout society is that people who enter the 12-Steps or a recovery community are alcoholics and drug addicts. This is nothing more than an incorrect stereotype. Most of the staff at HeartSupport has been through 12-Steps for issues such as self-hate, codependency, abandonment as a child, or pornography. Many of them sponsor men and women in their local communities going through similar issues or something completely opposite than they've gone through.

Many churches offer a spiritual version of the 12-Steps called Celebrate Recovery that seeks to help men and women process their "hurts, hang-ups, and habits." Many young men and women have entered the program specifically to begin the process of combating and overcoming self-harm with success.

Another resource you may consider is SMART Recovery. SMART participants learn tools for addiction recovery based on the latest scientific research and participate in a worldwide community that includes free, self-empowering, science-based mutual help groups. Like the 12-Steps and Celebrate Recovery, they offer a wide range of counseling for addictive behaviors.

A reason why recovery communities and 12-Step programs are so effective is they use many of the practices we shared earlier. They focus on a community going through similar issues, encourage vulnerability, and aren't having people in the group trying to "fix them."

A 12-Step or recovery community in your area might be the step you need to hold yourself accountable and begin to process on a deeper level in conjunction with this book and exercises. We highly encourage that step for all men and women reading this book as we've found massive freedom and healing not only in the staff members' lives at HeartSupport, but for other men and women who've gone through it as well.

Counseling/Professional Help

When people hear the word *counseling*, they sometimes

shudder. Most of the time, it's because that means we've finally realized the gravity of the situation. Admitting we need outside help for many is embarrassing—thus, we resist.

Sometimes friends and family members aren't equipped to handle severe cases of self-harm, and you'll need someone to dig into your life that can offer a third-party objective view. You'll be less inclined to think they're just being a jerk or don't know anything because it's coming from someone you haven't built a relationship with. Sometimes you'll be amazed at how much insight a stranger can suddenly have in your life. Because they're on the outside, they'll have a more concise view that can help.

The reality, however, is that there can still be resistance to the idea of counseling. Many people feel it's a sign of weakness. The alternative is far worse—staying stuck and struggling. It's important to recognize that not all counselors are created equal. Sometimes you'll need to check out more than one until you find the right fit and someone who meshes with your budget as well. I've known people who have gone through numerous counselors believing them worthless until they finally connected with the right one.

Begin by asking people you trust for recommendations and don't be limited by what you find on the internet. Perhaps the most important advice in choosing a counselor is choosing the relationship over their resume. If you visit with a few counselors and click with one who doesn't have the same level of accomplishments or reviews, go with the person you feel most comfortable with over their professional credentials.

> **Note for family and friends:** It will be essential for your loved one to choose a counselor they feel comfortable with, not one you think will help them the most.

As you can see, the process to recovery is long and requires commitment. Much of the process may seem overwhelming, but the exercises in the workbook section will give you a starting point to begin. Be forewarned! In order for progress to happen, it requires making the exercises a daily habit. You may be thinking it will be hard to form a new habit, but also remember self-injury is a habit you formed. It's possible to replace one with a healthier alternative if you're willing to commit to a new process.

To watch the accompanying videos that recap the chapter and provide a case study, visit http://heartsupport.com/SH

6

CAN FAITH AND SPIRITUALITY PLAY A ROLE IN HEALING?

How many people do you know who pray? Did you know there are atheists who pray? According to Pew Research 55 percent of Americans pray every day, and only 23 percent say they seldom or never pray, meaning a good chunk of the populace is interested in spiritual things.

While spirituality may seem strange to you, consider this for a moment: what was the most popular book series of the last decade? If you answered Harry Potter, you're correct. The novels focus on magic and the supernatural while combating evil forces in the universe. Men, women, and young adults desperately wanted to live inside that world, so much so that theme parks were built so people could experience Harry Potter's world.

While we may brush off the supernatural and spiritual as silly, there absolutely seems to be some part of human nature that craves it. So before you write off this chapter, take a moment to hear me out.

One of the problems our society has is that we're quick to come up with a streamlined solution for a complex problem. The solutions to self-harm have ranged from "they have a chemical imbalance, therefore they need medication" to "they need professional help" to "they need to pray more" to "they just need emotional support."

Human beings are complex. We are emotional, physical, and spiritual beings. When you reduce a problem to a single solution, you treat aspects of the person, rather than the whole. By only giving someone medication when they need a friend and prayer, you can completely invalidate and exacerbate the situation instead of helping them find healing.

Of the three hundred people we surveyed, more than half claimed spirituality and faith played a role in their recovery. That's a huge percentage for us to ignore just to avoid making someone feel uncomfortable about the topic. Even most recovery communities make use of claiming a higher power. For this chapter we'll be looking at key components of faith and spirituality that can help in the recovery process.

WHY FAITH?

Inside each and every person is a craving to truly be accepted for who we are, despite all our flaws and short-comings. For the person struggling with self-harm, the desire to be loved and understood despite the gravity of the situation is something we heard from almost every person we interviewed.

But here's where our society keeps missing a major

point with all these self-love/self-help books. Everywhere we look in our culture, we think that in order to overcome a struggle, especially in the secular mind-set, we need to first love and accept ourselves. If you love yourself and practice self-love, then you can overcome your feelings of inadequacy. What many of these books, though well-intentioned, fail to recognize is that you cannot get significance through self-recognition; it must come in great measure from others. This is perhaps most evident with the rise of social media. The more friends and followers we have, the more people like our content, then the better we feel about ourselves. Perhaps you've even seen young men and women reaching out to celebrities on social media begging them to follow them or respond, using drastic measures to grab their attention. Why would they do this?

Imagine for a moment your favorite artist is someone like Justin Bieber, Lady Gaga, Andy Biersack, or James Hetfield of Metallica. Suddenly out of all their followers they choose to respond and let you know explicitly that you matter. As a fan, your self-esteem and self-worth would skyrocket because of this simple fact—someone with a perceived greater worth gave you validation.

Dr. Timothy Keller explains this dilemma in one of his books where he states:

> In the end, you can't name yourself or bless yourself. You can't ultimately say to yourself, I don't care that everyone thinks I'm a monster. I love myself and that's all that matters. That would not convince us of our worth, unless we

were mentally unsound. We need someone from outside to say we are of great worth, and the greater the worth of the person telling us so, the more powerful that recognition is to our identity formation. So if we try to self-authenticate or validate ourselves, we place ourselves in an infinite loop of delusion that will lead to either narcissism or self-loathing.

This is one of the main reasons we encourage men and women to explore a higher power. If there is a God who is love and desires all his children to find hope and healing, then he would obviously be the ultimate source of validation. If he can never leave or forsake you, and believes you have infinite worth to him, then by having a higher power as the ultimate source of love, joy, and peace as your validation, you can truly begin to believe that you have worth and thus begin to combat self-harm.

Whereas, by seeking validation from another flawed human who can change their mind at a moment's notice, we'll always be left seeking out people's approval, never believing we are enough. But if there is a source that accepts us as we are, we can find infinite validation.

You may be saying, "All right, but which higher power? God, Jesus, Allah, Buddha? The Universe? Don't they all teach the same thing and why does it matter?"

FROM THE CHRISTIAN PERSPECTIVE

The community at HeartSupport is diverse. A little over half of our audience is Christian, while the other half is not. Because of this, we never want to shove our views down people's throats, but because the organization was founded on Christian principles, we give people the opportunity to explore and reach their own conclusions. As Dale Carnegie once stated, "A man convinced against his will, is of the same opinion still." So when people ask, "Can't my higher power be anything since they're all the same?" we like to give people fuel for thought and let them decide. We hope to do the same with you here if you're not a Christian, in a respectful manner, and then help you understand what this perspective would mean in terms of recovery from self-harm.

Throughout the major religions and philosophies of the world, you will indeed find almost identical teachings on topics regarding morality, such as these:

- Treat your neighbor as you would want to be treated.
- Don't steal.
- The path to life is through selflessness.
- Don't have sex with your neighbor's wife.

...and so on. However, when it comes to *who* God is and his nature, that's where the religions sharply divide. Buddhists believe there is no God, but that all life is suffering. In order to achieve Nirvana (enlightenment) and inner peace, we have to realize the illusion of life to escape the continuous cycles of reincarnation and suffering. Buddha, however, never claims to be God. He's just a man who taught this form of spiritual enlightenment.

Muslims believe that the way to get to God is through

following rules and the five pillars of Islam: prayer, concern for the needy, self-purification, fasting, and pilgrimage. By following the moral code and these teachings that were taught through the prophet Mohammed, you can reach paradise.

Hindus are very similar to Buddhists in that they believe this world is illusionary and worship numerous gods such as Shiva, Krishna, and Ganesh. Their gods have to be taken care of and appeased through a practice called "puja,"—by living a good life you can reach the next caste system.

Christianity, however, is the one world religion that teaches its founder is God, and that no amount of good works will earn you favor or save you. Jesus himself repeatedly states he is the way to eternal life and makes outrageous claims to divinity. Whereas all other major world religions teach something along the lines of "I'm a prophet or teacher who can lead you to God," Jesus teaches, "I'm God, come to find you." So while religions may all agree on moral ethics, it does nothing to help our situation of finding a higher source of love that validates us and accepts us in the midst of our struggle.

When we've brought this point up, the counterpoint is, "This is why we'll never have peace! Because none of the religions can get along and agree!"

To which we would state: you're correct. Religion will always divide and oppress. Because what is religion? Religion is a set of beliefs that guide you on how you interact in the world in its simplest form. Therefore, everyone has a "religion" they follow.

More often than not, religious beliefs tend to move

to oppression and violence. If you tell a group of people, "You have the truth and you are saved by performing that truth," such logic leads to feelings of superiority toward people who aren't performing the truth, and that in turn leads to a separation that causes you to pull away from the perceived impure people and become unfamiliar with them. At that point, you're able to believe the worst about them, judge them, create stereotypes, and inevitably oppress them either through marginalization or how you treat them.

We've met numerous men and women whose self-harm stems from being ostracized by the religious communities they were a part of. Because they weren't performing to the standard of their religion, they fell into despair and continued to injure.

But here's why Christianity is so different as a religion and where many in the Christian tradition have failed to communicate the truth in helping those struggling through self-harm.

Our goal is not to follow a set of rules to earn God's favor. If you believe that by not self-harming, God will love you more, that is a distorted version of the Christian message. What Jesus's teaching, death, and resurrection proclaim is that as good as we may try to be, we constantly fail and are in need of a savior to validate and provide our sense of worth.

Often, there are people out there who can easily live more moral lives than Christians do, but it is only through God's grace and his righteousness that we're saved, not because we self-harm or don't. If anything we realize what a train wreck we are, and so when we see people in this light, we are humbled. When we realize his great love for us despite our messiness, it attaches love, worth, purpose, and meaning to our existence. Other religions do not teach that premise.

You may be thinking, "That sounds nice in theory, but I sure do know a lot of Christians who judge and oppress and are responsible for some pretty horrific stuff." You would also be correct in this assessment. The French Enlightenment thinker Voltaire once quipped, "God made man in His own image, and ever since man has been returning the favor."

Voltaire is effectively saying that God made men and women in his image, and ever since, man has constantly tried to make God appear like a flawed man and not like God, thus warping his message. People can take any message in the world and distort it, and Christianity is no different. Many have used Jesus's teaching to divide, oppress, and conquer in the name of moral superiority.

I'm willing to bet at some point, maybe you had another Christian tell you what you're doing is evil and that self-harm was from the devil. Instead of offering you compassion, which is the nature and character of Jesus, you received shame and judgment. So who's right about you? Jesus? Or the person claiming to represent him that is oppressing others?

While men and women have distorted Jesus's teachings, the true message of Christianity has remained unchanged for two thousand years, and it's a simple message. God loves you right now, as is, whether you are in the clutches of self-harm or not, values you, believes you have infinite worth, and desires to have a relationship with you.

So what does this mean in terms of recovery and self-harm you may be asking?

Earlier I pointed out the problem with simply loving yourself when we derive meaning from those around us. But if you have a higher power whose message is that you are a masterpiece and wholly loved, that reality can begin to shift your perspective. If God did indeed create the world and everyone in it, only he would have the right to name and bless you, and if his nature is love, then by default you are infinitely loved.

Whereas other men and women will let you down or even tear you down, God promises he believes the best in you, even in the midst of self-harm, doubt, and relapse. Where you see failure, he sees opportunity for growth. Where you see addiction, he sees an opportunity to take a step. Where you've given up, he whispers, "You can make it."

What that tangibly looks like in recovery terms is surrendering truth over to a higher power. For instance, other chapters gave examples of how someone may cut themselves as a means of punishment. They believe lies about themselves and can think thoughts like, "I'm worthless, so I deserve this." When you surrender yourself to a higher power who believes you blameless and loved, or while you may not feel worthy, you choose to surrender that belief to a higher power and speak the higher power's truth over your life: "I am worthy because God believes I'm worthy and loved."

Last, we need to clarify that it is indeed possible to recover without a set of spiritual beliefs. Men and women for decades have used the 12-Steps and counseling to grow and recover from areas of trauma, struggle, and addiction. It would be naive to state that it's impossible to do without believing as we do. However, based on those who recover the fastest and have shared their experience, discovering or growing their faith has been paramount in the recovery process. We felt it necessary to include should you decide to explore more, including a series of videos on our website.

DOES PRAYER HELP?

Prayer may either seem silly to you—or essential. Scientifically, however, it has massive benefits for your recovery process. Research shows that it specifically has five benefits, according to Clay Routledge, a psychological scientist who writes in *Psychology Today*.

1. **Prayer increases self-control:** Right now, you feel you may have little self-control over when you injure yourself. Research participants discovered they exercised more self-control after prayer, even reducing the consumption of alcohol in one study. Prayer also has been shown to have an energizing effect, which can be vital when you feel hopeless about your situation.

2. **Prayer reduces anger:** Researchers found that people who pray reduced the amount of aggression they have and felt after a particularly anger-inducing incident. When struggling with self-injury you may be mad at yourself

or situations that caused you to injure. Prayer could help reduce those negative emotions and move you more toward peace.

3. **Prayer makes you a more forgiving person:** One of the major points those we surveyed addressed was that many had a hard time forgiving themselves for injuring. Research found that through prayer, you'll be more apt to forgive others and yourself.

4. **Prayer increases your ability to trust:** One of the key themes we pointed to in your recovery process is the ability to trust others and become vulnerable. Research shows that prayer increases unity and trust especially when done with another person. As you grow in trust, you'll be able to be more vulnerable with those around you and the struggle you're facing.

5. **Prayer can offset stress:** Another positive effect of prayer is that it can make you more resilient against the negative health effects of stress. Because self-injury is often a stressor for many people as they think and dwell on it, prayer could be a practice that helps reduce the amount of stress during your recovery.

Whether or not you feel comfortable praying, in the workbook section you'll discover a time of reflection you can use for critical self-improvement. Reflective self-awareness is a practice used by many people ranging from Christians, to Buddhists, to even great philosophers.

We believe this will help you progress in your recovery the more self-aware you become.

READING SACRED LITERATURE

My God, my God, why have you forsaken me?

Why are you so far from saving me,

so far from my cries of anguish?

My God, I cry out by day, but you do not answer,

by night, but I find no rest.
(Psalm 22:1–2)

In antiquity, King David was known as a warrior and a poet. The Book of Psalms features some of his poems, laments, and praises for God during the events going on in his life. A common misconception about the Bible is that it's an instruction booklet on how to live a moral life, when that is the furthest thing from the truth.

The over-arching theme of the Bible is man's repeated failures, and the story of God's intervention to ransom and show his love for creation. The Bible's sacred literature features men and women of questionable backgrounds and repeated moral failings and God's great love using those who stumble the most.

In the text you'll read stories of anguish, asking where God is in the midst of pain and hurt, or outright doubt and disbelief. Other times you'll find encouraging and comforting words from those who have experienced the hardest moments life has to offer. If you will keep a view of the theme of redemption throughout your reading, you just might view the Bible and its sacred literature in a different light that proves to be a soothing balm during your recovery process.

If you're looking for a place to begin, we recommend the Book of John and reading about the life of Jesus and how he interacts with those struggling.

A FAITH COMMUNITY

One of the things you may be noticing by this point is how much we at HeartSupport believe in the power of community to create change. In the chapter on recovery, we looked at the reason why volunteering or joining a community can be essential to your recovery. By surrounding yourself with like-minded individuals who share the same faith as you, you'll be more apt to begin taking proactive steps and sharing with others so that they can help carry some of the burden as well as pray for you.

However, I must add an important warning. Not all faith communities are created equal. Just like my wife Emily's water glass story I referenced, trust needs to be established first. The people within the community need to be practicing the values of empathy and compassion outlined in the chapter for friends and family members.

Sadly, sometimes those within faith communities can be the most judgmental because of a fundamental misunderstanding of how their faith should compel them to help others. That being said, as trust and vulnerability begin to develop, you'll find supporters who can pray and encourage you in your faith, which can be vital toward your healing.

A FINAL NOTE

I realize that some (or even many) of you view faith and spirituality with a bit of pain and resistance. You may have even been the victim of spiritual abuse or sexual abuse at the hands of clergy, so grasping any of the ideas I've laid out seems impossible. We at HeartSupport want you to know we understand and can only apologize on behalf of those who've misrepresented what we believe to be a loving and grace-filled God.

Some of our own staff and people on our website's community forum have been victims of the same travesties. We ask that this section doesn't taint your view toward the whole of recovery and that even without this section, we know if you put to practice the steps laid out, big changes can happen.

To watch the accompanying videos that recap the chapter and provide a case study, visit http:// heartsupport.com/SH

If you're interested in exploring more on the subject of spirituality and faith visit http://heartsupport. com/explore

7

RELAPSE

(Happens to the Best of Us)

One thing that has helped me heal is just knowing someone is always there for me in the time I need them. And if I happen to relapse and go to someone about it, it's nice to feel like I'm not being judged for harming myself. Most times all I need is a person to hug me and listen because I honestly don't know what to say after a relapse. Just that it happened. Talking through what triggers me also helps me in my recovery. The person I'm talking to often gives me new perspective to think about that I didn't see before. —Madeleine

Ben Haggerty found himself in rehab in the summer of 2008 for drug and alcohol addiction. But after a few years of sobriety, he began working on his music passions and soon found himself touring with a growing audience. In 2014, his album won a Grammy and he had a handful of number-one singles. He was even engaged to be married. But that was also when he started slipping.

"I held it together for a while," he said. "But, eventually, I stopped going to my 12-Step meetings. I was burned out. I was superstressed. I just wanted to escape."

And that's exactly what he did. During South by Southwest Music Festival his fiancée found pills in his shoes, and he soon found himself bargaining with sobriety and hiding it from others: "I would tell myself Monday, I'ma stop…OK. Tuesday, I'ma stop…OK…I might as well go on to the weekend. Sunday, I'm done. But after this bag of weed…"

Ben found himself in full-blown relapse, and it wasn't until he stepped back into his 12-Step community that he was able to combat the shame he felt and find himself on the path to recovery again. He even wrote a song about the process of relapse and recovery entitled "Starting Over."

But perhaps you might know him better by his stage name: Macklemore.

RELAPSE HAPPENS TO THE BEST OF US

Recovery is hardly a straight line. Imagine it instead like a challenging mountain path full of obstacles.

If you've ever participated in a Tough Mudder or a Spartan Race, you probably understand just how difficult certain obstacles can be. There's a freezing ice bath and even electrocution near the end of the Tough Mudder, all while trudging through grueling terrain for ten or more miles.

One obstacle in particular is called Everest 2.0. It looks like a skateboard ramp in appearance but is a slick quarter pipe over fifteen feet tall. The recurved top makes it extra hard to get a handhold in order to get over the obstacle. What you'll typically see is people running full speed at the wall grasping for the top only to slide down over and over, all the while dragging more mud on the wall making it slicker and more difficult to conquer.

Relapse is like that wall. It's common most people won't get over the obstacle without falling at least once, but it isn't failure. Failure only happens when you stop trying. However, the whole process of running up the proverbial wall only to slide to the bottom again can be extremely frustrating.

At the Everest wall you'll see hordes of men and women at the base who haven't made it over and have fallen down a few times. According to researchers writing in the *Journal of the American Medical Association*, just like the men and women struggling to get over the wall who have fallen, up to 60 percent of recovery patients endure a relapse. In some cases, it can be as high as 75 percent.

A relapse, however, is often the period of greatest growth and can lay the groundwork for complete freedom. The fall may help strengthen your resolve to get up and try once more. While you may feel tired and beat up, it can be a sign to modify your strategy or point to areas you've let slack that need new boundaries enforced.

There is no shame in relapse. The only shame you'll experience will be self-induced for not trying again.

SIGNS YOU'RE HEADED FOR A RELAPSE

Warning signs help us discover potential danger ahead. Restaurant menus will often mark whether a product contains allergens. Flashing signs may indicate an upcoming hazard on the road. Even your body will give you warnings when you push yourself too hard at the gym.

In the process of your recovery from self-injury, watch for warning signs that might help you avoid a relapse.

1. **Old Haunts and Triggering Scenarios:** If it walks like a duck and quacks like a duck, you can bet it's a duck. If you found yourself injuring in a certain environment or surrounded by things that can trigger memories, there's a good probability that the more you're in those scenarios or situations, the more you'll be apt to relapse. It's best to avoid people and places that were part of your old habit, and instead develop a new schedule or a community of people committed to your recovery. Additionally, avoid glorifying your story of self-harm. If you find yourself minimizing the effects it had on your life when sharing with others, it can be a trigger or a warning sign.

2. **Stress or Difficult Life Events:** While everyone experiences pain and suffering in their life, how we all deal with it is different. Some people numb it with social media or shopping, but in your case, injuring is the mechanism you may use to cope with a hard day. Getting

dumped, fired, a bad grade, or experiencing loss can happen to us all. When stress and life events accumulate, we can have a tendency to throw up our hands and say, "It's too much! I need a release!" Don't buy into the lie. Press in and continue working at this book and the steps laid out for you. This too shall pass.

3. **Talking about Relapsing:** A surefire way to spot an imminent relapse is if you keep talking about it or all the "glory days" when you used to injure. If you start posing "what-if" scenarios to others, it's a bad sign. In these moments, take a step back and remind yourself of the numerous negative aspects and the cost of injuring yourself, and then begin shifting your conversation and recovery tactics to healthier subjects.

4. **An Overly Confident Attitude:** This is one we see often. A guy or girl will begin to make steps and find freedom. Life is going well and there are major changes happening. Then they get cocky about it. "Man, this feels so great! I don't see how I could ever go back to injuring!" They remove the boundaries they had put in place and stop working their recovery because they think they can handle their cravings to injure without them. Without fail, they head straight into relapse and are dumbfounded when it happens. Part of recovery is having the humility to recognize you need help. It's also recognizing recovery takes time until you have

fully recovered. Don't lose site of the summit
to stop and marvel at how far you've gone and
decide to stop there. Keep climbing.

5. **Becoming Defensive and Returning to a Pattern of Denial:** If you remember Macklemore's
story, his relapse began with denial—"Okay
just this once." If you've told yourself, "Just this
once," and injured, you probably know you're
sliding into old patterns again. You'll typically
become defensive with your friends, family,
and community. A defensive position to those
trying to love and care about you should be
a warning bell that you're headed into full-
blown relapse and are damaging your recovery
efforts.

TECHNIQUES FOR DEALING WITH URGES OF RELAPSE

In recovery there's a common phrase many people use:
"One day at a time." Right now, you may be wondering
whether you can stay clean forever, and that can feel
overwhelming. The first thing you need to remember is
just getting through today. When tomorrow rolls around,
focus on recovery for that day. But if you begin feeling the
urge to injure strongly, these techniques may help.

- Tell someone you're thinking about injuring.
  Remember what we talked about in the recovery
  process that having a community and installing
  several forms of feedback is vital to recovery.

When you feel that urge, reaching out to someone you trust and talking through your feelings
can monumentally decrease the urge to injure.

- Distract yourself. Calling a friend or your
  accountability partner is one step to distract
  yourself, but what if they're not available? One of
  the best things you can do is go somewhere busy
  where it's next to impossible to injure without
  creating a scene. Head to a busy coffee shop
  or the mall. Put on gym clothes and head out
  for a run. Most urges only last fifteen to thirty
  minutes at a time, so keep busy to head off your
  chances.

- Play out the scenario in your head. When you
  begin to feel the urge to injure, play out what
  would happen if you did it again. Most urges
  would have you believe it's "just this once," like I
  stated earlier. But the practice of playing out all
  the consequences and how you would feel can be
  a starting point for stopping. Remind yourself of
  the negative consequences you've already faced,
  and how much more it impedes your growth.

WHEN IT'S *NOT* RELAPSE

Over the years we've met a lot of men and women
struggling not just with self-harm, but substance abuse,
codependency, or a pornography addiction.

A phrase we often hear from them is: "I relapsed."

For some people, it is indeed relapse. For many we've

met, however, it's not. What exactly is meant by that?

People like recovery terminology because it gives them a starting point. They feel as if they're on the road to getting better. But sometimes it's an excuse to choose your addiction while putting a term on it that doesn't make you feel so bad. If you relapse every day for a year, is it relapse? Or are you just an addict choosing your addiction?

In order for a relapse to occur, you have to be actively participating in recovery. I cannot stress this enough. If you read this book and learn how to recover but don't apply it and continue to injure, you're not in relapse when you harm yourself. You're still choosing destructive tendencies only with a greater knowledge of how you're doing them.

If you're not making proactive steps to change your situation, then you're not relapsing or even in recovery. As hard as it may be to hear, you're still in the same spot you've always been. Take a moment to decide whether or not you're going to commit to the recovery process, and proceed accordingly. At least you'll be honest enough with yourself to know whether you're going to put forth the effort or not.

WHAT TO DO IF YOU RELAPSE

When or if you relapse, you may have the thought, "I knew I couldn't do it. And now there's nothing to do about it but just embrace the failure." We cannot stress enough that relapse is not failure, but a growing opportunity. One shower on Monday does not clean the grime gained on a Wednesday. It is a daily practice of self-care that needs daily attention and maintenance (like healthy eating and exercise).

Some days are harder than others, and being aware of this and not expecting perfection helps. Relapse will be hard to face because of the amount of guilt or shame you may feel. But just remember what we talked about in our chapter about guilt and shame, or go back and review it. Part of the process of recovering will be speaking to those messages of shame you tell yourself while developing a sense of resiliency throughout the process with each victory and setback.

The best thing you can do is harness the power of your story. Okay, so you relapsed. Now what? Is this how your story ends? Defeated and halfway through the journey? Or do you make it to the mountaintop and claim victory after getting busted up and a little battered?

Make it to the mountaintop.

To watch the accompanying videos that recap the chapter and provide a case study, visit http:// heartsupport.com/SH

8

YOU'RE NOT CRAZY, SICK, OR DOOMED TO STAY STUCK

If you're struggling with self-harm, you need to understand one thing clearly: You're not crazy or doomed to this forever.

If you're a parent of a loved one or a friend of someone who self-injures, you need to understand, they're not sick.

That may sound like irresponsible, irrational talk, but hear me out for a second.

Throughout history men and women have coped with emotional pain or trauma in a variety of ways. Some turn to the bottle, some to pills, some to excessive exercise, while others turn to new and inventive ways of coping that are healthy (The Whole30 diet, for example, was started by a former heroin addict.). Unfortunately, for most, their creative ways of coping end up being destructive.

One summer, one of our staff members, Nate, met a girl named Sarah who struggled with an eating disorder. As Nate sat listening, she remarked, "I'm sick, as you know, and I just don't think I'll ever get better."

Nate, who had been through recovery himself, knew exactly where she was coming from because this was one of his biggest fears. He was afraid that his desire to use would never fade, and these addictive "itches" would always be there. He was afraid that his best hope in recovery was to learn to get really good at not scratching the constant and consuming itch.

One day, however, his mentor told him something that changed his perspective and gave him hope. He pulled Nate aside and said, "You know, Nate, your addiction isn't your problem."

Nate was taken aback at first. His addiction was the reason he had been meeting one-on-one with his mentor for the past nine months! It was the reason he'd gone through all of the work to recover. What his mentor ended up explaining, however, was that his "addiction was his solution to a deeper problem he was facing."

Nate realized his addiction was actually an emotional Band-Aid for when he felt overwhelmed or upset or when things weren't going his way (much how someone who self-injures feels). He used the addiction as a way to escape and check out of pain he experienced in life.

So when Nate heard Sarah share about her life, instead of viewing her as sick or doomed to struggle endlessly, he had hope that she could change.

Sarah grew up with addict parents who loved her unpredictably. She never knew if it was going to be a good day where they were sober and coherent or if it was going to be a bad one where they would fly off the handle at the littlest thing she did. She felt like love was scary because love was unpredictable. She never knew whether love meant getting beaten or getting hugged. She desperately lacked and wanted control. And she found that control in her image.

By controlling the way she looked, she could predictably receive compliments and "love" from others. It was her way to regain the power, the control, that she felt she didn't have growing up. So when she felt unloved or sad or pain, she stopped eating because it felt as if she was taking proactive steps toward receiving love. And in that sense, when you reveal the roots of her addiction and see it for what it truly is, you see that it's actually a creative solution to a significant problem she faced in her past.

When Nate pointed that out to her, he told her: "Sarah, you're not sick. You're just logical," and something clicked for Sarah when she heard that. She realized that if her addiction wasn't some terminal illness that would be with her forever—if her addiction was just one way she solved her problems—maybe she could find a better way to deal with the pain in her life. Maybe she could recover. Maybe she wasn't doomed to anorexia for the rest of her life. Maybe her life could be filled with happiness and hope and purpose and excitement.

As Nate watched the hope fill her face when she realized the logic in his statement, he recognized there's something wrong with the way some traditional schools of thought view recovery.

The two main schools of thought in recovery are typically as follows:

1. The "you are sick" school says you need to take

these pills, attend these meetings, follow these rules, and hopefully be able to corral your impulses.

2. The "you are logical" school says you are responsible for uncovering the source of your addictions, figuring out what the hurt is underneath your problems, healing from that past wound, and learning new ways to cope with pain moving forward. It demands for you to create better habits instead of just getting better and managing your bad habits. It requires you to learn and set your foundation on sound and helpful long-term principles and not quick-fix behavioral-management Band-Aids that end up causing infection and worse problems in your life than the original ones it claimed to heal.

If you struggle with self-harm, you may have remarked just as Sarah did, "I'm sick and I can't get any better." Maybe a parent, friend, or loved one has even reinforced this mentality with comments like these: "You're always going to be this way" or "What's wrong with you that you do this?"

The reality is that whatever your reason for self-harming—whether known or unknown to you—self-harm is nothing more than an inventive and logical response to something else (a feeling of control, to feel better, or many of the other reasons we've covered in this book). You're not terminally sick, you're just seeking a way to heal that's ultimately been destructive as opposed to helpful.

The good news, then, is that your journey with self-harm is less of a symbol of struggle and more a symbol of strength. You had the strength to solve the pain in your life once; now you have a new pain, and we are confident you'll be able to solve this too. You are creative, and you are logical. You will find a new way out, and we at HeartSupport hope this resource will help guide you on this healthier path. Remember you are in the middle of this journey, and with each day you become ever closer to your summit. We believe you will rewrite the end of your story, and it will be a beautiful one of trial, but then triumph, indeed.

To watch the accompanying videos that recap the chapter and provide a case study, visit http:// heartsupport.com/SH

9

I'M A FRIEND/FAMILY MEMBER. HOW CAN I HELP?

B eing heard is so close to being loved that for
the average person, they are almost indistin-
guishable. —David Augsburger

If you're someone struggling with self-harm, you might
think you should skip this chapter. However, I would
encourage you not to do that as you may learn ways in
which to engage with your friends, loved ones, or family
members to help them understand your struggle more
effectively and ways to respond.

If you're a friend wanting to know how to ask questions
and engage, you'll learn the best practices in this chapter.

If you're a family member wanting to know signs to
look for or how to practice empathy and compassion
when the entire situation has been nothing but frustrating, then you definitely need to read on.

"WHAT COULD I HAVE DONE TO PREVENT THIS?"

The first question so many friends and family members want to know is a simple one: "What could I have done to prevent this?"

Many parents or friends can spend hours retracing things they've said or actions they've done. They unproductively rehash episodes in their minds and blame events and peers for the reason a child or friend started self-injury.

Whether you're experiencing worry, sadness, anger, or other emotions, it's totally normal. You're not crazy for wishing you could have done something to make your loved one's life better.

Here's the good news: you have that opportunity to make a positive difference, but focusing on regret would be a waste of this key moment. We'll teach you some effective tactics in this chapter, but it starts with your decision to be an advocate. Will you do what it takes to be emotionally available for your daughter or son? Will you commit to honoring their vulnerability and seeking to understand your friend? Will you choose to believe in them and in their success throughout this process?

Everything else we teach is dependent on your heart and the decision you make here. If you're ready, then we can get started.

LISTEN FIRST

Every guy can recall the time when they were asked to

repeat back word-for-word what their spouse or girlfriend said. What's amazing is they can typically repeat the basic gist of what their loved one said or perhaps even the full conversation.

But the next words that leave your significant other's mouth are: "You're just not hearing me!"

Stephen Covey, in his book *The 7 Habits of Highly Effective People*, lists habit number five as "Seek first to understand, then to be understood." Listening is something many of us don't do well. More often than not we want to be understood so we can get our point across. A lot of times when someone is talking, we may be already formulating a response in our head, grabbing key parts of the conversation, only to miss the meaning entirely.

When you listen to reply, you end up not fully understanding or empathizing. You can even devalue the discussion by injecting your experience in it when you decide what the other person means before he or she finishes communicating.

Have you ever said the following? "Oh, I know just how you feel. I felt the same way." "I had the same thing happen to me." "Let me tell you what I did in a similar situation."

Covey explains that we often listen "autobiographically" and tend to respond in one of four ways:

Evaluating: You judge and then either agree or disagree.
Probing: You ask questions from your own frame of reference.
Advising: You give counsel, advice, and solutions

to problems.

Interpreting: You analyze others' motives and behaviors based on your own experiences.

Covey goes on to explain that there may be resistance to hearing these autobiographical messages because, after all, you're just trying to help by drawing on your own experiences and relate. While it may be appropriate in some responses, such as friends or family members who have also struggled with self-harm, most times instead of seeking to understand another's point of view, you're stacking it up against a personal resume, and it negates what they're feeling. Most couples that end up in a counselor's office, for instance, typically mutter these words: "He (she) just doesn't listen to me!"

When dealing with someone who's struggling through self-harm, you must first establish trust by asserting you're simply there to listen—and never to judge. If you've ever attended a 12-Step meeting, one of the rules essential toward recovery and safety is when someone in the group shares you do not respond with life advice or try to fix their situation. It's a time for them to share their hurts, emotions, and hang-ups.

Learning to communicate effectively begins by listening. When you listen and empathize in an active manner with someone else, it shows you love them and care about what they have to say and what they're feeling. Even if it doesn't make sense to you.

EMPATHY

Just what exactly is empathy? What separates it from sympathy? And just how can you practice empathy with someone struggling through self-injury?

A nursing scholar named Theresa Wiseman published a widely circulated article in the *Journal of Advanced Nursing* entitled "A concept analysis of empathy" that was the first of its kind to identify key attributes when practicing empathy. In her article she breaks down empathy into four simple, yet defining attributes. In studying her work, we discovered her work also aligned with the best practices in listening as well. Wiseman defines the four elements of empathy as follows:

1. To see the world as others see it (the opposite of advising)
2. To be nonjudgmental (the opposite of evaluating)
3. Understanding another's feelings (the opposite of interpreting)
4. Communicating understanding of another's feelings (the opposite of probing)

Let's take a look at each of these attributes for a moment and examine how we can apply them to empathizing with someone going through self-harm—even if we personally haven't been through it.

To See the World as Others See It
We've all probably heard the phrase, "You can't under-

stand someone until you've walked a mile in their shoes." This, however, can prove difficult in empathizing with a loved one if you feel they're making mistakes or life decisions you disagree with, particularly in the case of self-harm.

Empathy here requires that you suspend your personal beliefs and ideologies to imagine the world through how someone struggling with self-harm views it. You're effectively trying to look at the events in their life through their eyes, not your own. When you're able to do that, you can offer compassion and understanding even if self-harm is something you haven't experienced. It will also help you understand why they do it as well.

To Be Nonjudgmental

Often when we hear about something we disagree with—whether morally, politically, intellectually, or spiritually—we're quick to cast judgment. Everyone will judge something or someone in their life. It's a pattern we do subconsciously that most times we aren't even aware of. When we judge people, it's often a reflection of our own beliefs and values.

The quickest way to invalidate someone struggling through self-harm is to judge them based on their actions. Saying things like, "This just didn't happen when I was growing up," or "What's wrong with you that this is your response to emotional pain?" completely invalidates and discounts the hurt a person is feeling. It's often an attempt to protect ourselves from the awkwardness and pain of the situation.

Because we love to compare ourselves to others we feel

are falling short or we believe are making poor decisions, it can puff us up to believe we're making better decisions and therefore cast judgment. However, none of us would compare ourselves to Jesus, Mother Teresa (now Saint Teresa), or Gandhi, as we would fall very short. In order to practice empathy and compassion, we must suspend judgment.

Understanding Another's Feelings

This point goes back to active listening that I spoke of earlier in the chapter. In order to practice this effectively, we must be aware of our own feelings and emotions to understand another's. We must put our own emotions about the situation to the side to provide emotional first aid for the person struggling.

If we are unable to recognize the difference between fear and disappointment in our own lives, then we'll often miss the subtleties in others' emotions as well. We must ask ourselves questions like, "Are they afraid or just angry? Feeling worthless or abandoned?" Diving to the heart of their (and your) emotions will help all the more to relate to the man or woman struggling.

Communicating Understanding of Another's Feelings

This is the most difficult step in practicing empathy. If we miss hearing and feeling what the person battling self-harm is trying to communicate, our response can miss the mark rather than help.

When communicating with someone struggling with self-injury it's vital to reflect that you understand what they're feeling. Instead of saying something like, "You're depressed and anxious, so that's why you're cutting?" you want to replace the sentiment with how they feel. That may look something like, "It sounds like you feel every day is a constant battle you're not winning, and cutting is the only option to release the internal pain."

When they feel you understand their pain and heartache, they'll begin to see you truly care as well.

AFFIRMATION

A key to practicing empathy is affirming a self-injurer when they take small steps to share or become vulnerable. What this helps do is tell them, "I hear you and I understand." By affirming them, you help validate their feelings and experiences, which gives them the courage to share more in the future and take proactive steps toward recovery because they feel supported.

As they take steps, it's vital to point out they're making progress, no matter how small. The hope and mental fortitude such affirmation gives them can empower them to make more positive changes and prevent discouragement. Affirming statements can look like any of the following:

- "Thank you so much for sharing and being open about this. I imagine that must have been scary to share something as vulnerable as what you're going through."
- "The steps you've been taking are impressive. I realize you don't think they're that big, but these things add up over time, and it shows your hard

work and dedication."

The more you affirm their progress and positive inter-actions, the more it helps them feel safe and cared for.

AVOIDING ARGUMENTS AND SETTING BOUNDARIES

It's tempting to engage in arguments with someone who's injuring especially if they become hostile, defiant, or provocative. If you try to "fix" their circumstance or convince them they have to change, it can immediately put them on the defensive.

Just remember someone has to *want* to change first, only then can progress be made. Your entire goal is to listen and reflect empathy until they begin to see the need to change themselves.

But what happens if you've been empathetic and listened for quite some time and they refuse to change?

Rolling with Resistance

Let's say a friend or family member has become defiant. Maybe they view self-harm as not a big deal after months of listening and asking questions. Perhaps they roman-ticize it. Resistance can mean it's time to shift tactics or listen in a new way to offer feedback.

The key to doing this, however, is remaining non-judgmental and respectful. Remember, we want to avoid arguments. Be very, very careful, however. Using this too early when your loved one is depressed can do more dam-age than a perspective shift. Use wisdom and discernment as to the time when to approach them with this method.

The key to rolling with your loved one's resistance is this: offer amplified reflection. Amplified reflection (sometimes called motivational interviewing) may look like this:

> Self-Injurer: "I don't see what the big deal is! I can quit whenever I want! This just helps me cope with stress."
> Friend/Parent: "So if I asked your friends, most of them would agree it's not a big deal? Is that correct?"

The point is not to do it with sarcasm, but to reflect their exaggerated claim. This helps avoid arguments by inviting new perspectives and still treating the person nonjudgmentally and with respect. It also helps them realize just how ridiculous their claims may be when it comes out of the mouth of someone else. By using their resistance, you help address their resistance and hopefully divert it toward positive change.

Setting Boundaries

While all this sounds good in theory, if you're a parent or a friend who's had a history of trying to help—but only ends up getting blamed—this can sound counterproductive.

You may be saying, "*Please.* I've tried this and they continue to lash out." Practicing empathy and listening does not mean that you just love them blindly and hope for the best. No parent lets their toddler grab a bottle of

Drano and then says, "I love them enough to respect their decisions, and I hope this works out for them." Nor would you stand motionless if you saw a bus heading for an unsuspecting stranger standing in the middle of the road. That wouldn't be loving or practicing empathy.

Sometimes the most loving thing you can do is let someone experience the consequences of their actions to provoke change. Creating firm but loving boundaries helps them understand the consequences of their actions. If you're a parent, that may mean explaining until they've put in the time to work recovery, there will be restrictions imposed. If you're a friend, it may mean explaining that until they begin to take steps toward healing, you can't listen to them complain about constantly struggling. The conversation moving forward will be off-limits.

Remember, boundaries help keep others accountable and within their limits without destroying yours.

HOW CAN I APPROACH (WITHOUT SCARING THEM OFF)?

Imagine you see your favorite movie actor on the street and you want to say hello. However, fear rises in your gut, and you remain paralyzed, say nothing, and miss your opportunity. A lot of people feel similar when they wonder how to approach a family member or friend struggling with self-harm. They're afraid they'll get irrationally upset and may do more damage than good. But at the same time they don't want to just let them stay stuck, and yet feel paralyzed to do anything about it for lack of experience.

I won't lie. This is often the hardest and scariest step—

the initial contact and revelation that you know their secret can be off-putting. One of our team members uses a tactic in conflict resolution he learned from his parents. When someone joins his team, he lets them know, "You are welcome to tell me anything, just remember it's all in how you say it."

Going back to the practice of listening and empathy, a best first step to break the ice without scaring them off is simply this: Let the person who self-harms know that you want to listen to them and hear how they are feeling when they feel ready and able to talk about it. Give them some space and time to reflect and think about what you've told them. Don't expect an immediate response, and be prepared for them to be upset. Remember, you've just uncovered and made them aware you know of one of their deepest secrets and sources of shame. Anger can often be a natural reaction when something you've done in private is brought to light.

Another way to approach them is with a handwritten letter letting them know you care and want to talk when they're ready. This may help you formulate your thoughts and revise sentences to make your words more soothing and empathetic.

WHAT ARE SOME SIGNS TO LOOK FOR IF YOU SUSPECT SELF-INJURY?

Since there numerous ways in which a person can injure themselves, we've kept this list to the most common and what we've seen from experience and other researchers.

- Cuts, scratches, or burns on the wrists, arms, legs, thighs, back, hips, or stomach
- Wearing loose clothing or always wearing long sleeves or pants even during hot days (commonly we'll often see young men and women in hoodies at concerts we attend even when the weather is in the high nineties)
- Constantly making excuses for cuts, burns, marks, or wounds on their body ("I cut myself cooking." "It's a sport injury.")
- Bruises that never seem to heal
- Hair loss or bald spots
- Repeated broken bones
- Claiming to have frequent accidents or mishaps that cause an injury
- Finding razors, scissors, lighters, knives, or blades in odd places (for instance: finding razor blades in a child's nightstand, drawer, or under their bed)
- Spending long time periods locked in their bedroom or bathroom
- An unhealthy desire to be alone, isolated, or avoid social situations
- Wearing numerous wristbands covering a good portion of their arm (we see this also at concerts in order to hide cuts on their wrists without wearing long sleeves)

WHAT *NOT* TO DO

If you're a parent, it can be devastating to discover that

your child is involved in deliberately injuring themselves. Your emotions have or will probably range from anger to tears to rage to disbelief to wanting to rescue them. If you're a friend, the emotions can be very similar to that of a parent. However, if you rush in too quickly and react inappropriately and respond out of those emotions, you can scare them off or damage the relationship.

Here's a list of actions experts recommend not doing that will only make the person feel ostracized, invalidated, or shamed.

- Do not stare at their scars. This may be difficult especially if they're fresh wounds or particularly disturbing, but they're looking for acceptance in that moment, and they're already keenly aware of their scars.

- Do not judge them. This should go without saying as I've covered the reasons why earlier, but for the sake of clarity, when you judge someone who self-harms, it produces more shame and makes them less apt to heal.

- Do not try to "fix it." While well-intentioned, there is a process to help heal from this, and overreacting and trying to fix it immediately (such as in-patient holds) actually break down your relationship. If someone is at immediate risk of hurting themselves or others (suicide), that is different. Developing trust and rapport is essential first before making suggestions.

- Do not ask them what they used to cut or harm

themselves. This question can be particularly triggering for someone and reminds them of why they did it, therefore increasing the urge to do it once more.

- Do not tell them, "You have to promise that you won't do it again." It's not as simple as making a promise. If it were, they could simply use their own willpower and promises to stop. Many boyfriends, girlfriends, or spouses will say this believing that if they truly love them, they'll stop the behavior. Remember, recovery is a process.

- Do not tell them, "But you're so pretty (handsome). Why would you do this to yourself?" Flaws don't take away beauty. Some people who self-harm use the body image issues as a reason to self-harm. This response can often provoke continued self-hatred.

- Do not assume the self-harm is for attention or aesthetic. Don't treat them as if they're crazy or trying to kill themselves either.

Last, if you can remember one thing and one thing only, it's to listen empathetically with an open mind, and love them regardless of how messy the situation. Their greatest chance for recovery stems from a loving community and family committed to helping them connect and belong in a safe environment. The more vulnerable you are in opening up your life to them, the more they will trust you. Trust begets trust. Empathy reveals compassion. And compassion begins to heal wounds.

END NOTES

For more information on self-harm, and to clarify and document the excellent research cited in this book, please peruse these sources. Websites are accurate as of publication but are subject to change, as are all addresses on the internet.

Chapter 1
National Alliance on Mental Illness, "Self-Harm," www.nami.org/Learn-More/Mental-Health-Conditions/Related-Conditions/Self-harm.

Michael Hollander, *Helping Teens Who Cut*, Guilford Press, 2008, p. 15.

Loretta G. Breuning, "Self-Harm in Animals: What We Can Learn From It," Psychology Today, www.psychologytoday.com/blog/your-neurochemical-self/201305/self-harm-in-animals-what-we-can-learn-it.

Tracy Alderman, *The Scarred Soul: Understanding and Ending Self-Inflicted Violence*, New Harbinger Publications, 1997.

A 2006 study in Pediatrics estimates that nearly one in five college students have deliberately injured themselves at least once. It should also be noted that when Heart-Support surveyed over 300 men and women, many had injured well into their twenties and others were still injuring despite being in their thirties.

Carrie Arnold, October 13, 2014, "Why Self-Harm?" Aeon, https://aeon.co/essays/how-self-harm-provokes-the-brain-into-feeling-better.

P. L. Kerr, J. J. Muehlenkamp, and J. M. Turner (2010), "Nonsuicidal Self-injury: A Review of Current Research for Family Medicine and Primary Care Physicians," *Journal of the American Board of Family Medicine* 23(2), 240–59.

Sarah Marsh, March 1, 2017, "A Quarter of Young Men Self-harm to Cope with Depression, Says Survey," The Guardian, www.theguardian.com/society/2017/mar/01/quarter-of-young-men-self-harm-cope-depression-poll.

Chapter 2
Andrew Perrin, "Social Media Usage: 2005–2015," Pew Research Center, October 8, 2015, www.pewinternet.org/2015/10/08/social-networking-usage-2005-2015/.

Susannah Fox and Sydney Jones, "Depression, Anxiety, Stress or Mental Health Issues, Pew Research Center, June 11, 2009, www.pewinternet.org/2009/06/11/depression-anxiety-stress-or-mental-health-issues/.

Chapter 3
Matthew K. Nock and Mitchell J Prinstein (2004), "A Functional Approach to the Assessment of Self-Mutilative Behavior," *Journal of Consulting and Clinical Psychology* 72(5), 885–90, www.people.fas.harvard.edu/~nock/nock-lab/Nock_Prinstein_JCCP2004.pdf.

Tori DeAngelis, "A New Look at Self-injury," American Psychological Association, July/August 2015, www.apa.org/monitor/2015/07-08/self-injury.aspx.

Chapter 4
Brené Brown, *Daring Greatly: How the Courage to Be Vulnerable Transforms the Way We Live, Love, Parent, and Lead*, Gotham Books, 2012.

Chapter 5
Steven Pressfield, *The War of Art: Break Through the Blocks and Win Your Inner Creative Battles*, Black Irish Entertainment, 2012.

Johann Hari is a journalist who began researching the war on drugs only to discover something immensely fascinating. His discoveries led to a well-known TED Talk entitled "Everything you think you know about addiction is wrong, www.ted.com/talks/johann_hari_everything_you_think_you_know_about_addiction_is_wrong.

Chapter 6
Michael Lipka, "5 Facts about Prayer," Pew Research

Center, May 4, 2016, www.pewresearch.org/fact-tank/2016/05/04/5-facts-about-prayer/.

Timothy Keller, *Preaching: Communicating Faith in an Age of Skepticism*, Penguin, 2015.

Portions of this chapter have been adapted from sermons, teachings, or the personal instruction the author received from Dr. Timothy Keller, John Burke, Leonce Crump II, and Matt Chandler. For more we invite you to read Dr. Keller's best-selling novel *The Reason for God* to discover more.

Curious about God? We have a series of videos on our website exploring questions of faith ranging from suffering to science. You can watch them at http://heartsupport.com/explore.

Clay Routledge, "5 Scientifically Supported Benefits of Prayer," Psychology Today, June 23, 2014, www.psychologytoday.com/blog/more-mortal/201406/5-scientifically-supported-benefits-prayer.

The book of Lamentations is Jeremiah's lament to God. Job asks God why pain and suffering has befallen him when he's lived an upright life. King David has repeated moral failures and is often found wondering where God is in the Psalms. Jesus, before going to the cross is riddled with fear and anxiety to the point he sweats blood. And finally, after the resurrection of Jesus Christ, his own disciple, Thomas, doubts any of it has happened until he can put his hands in the wounds.

Chapter 7

Complex Magazine, "Find a Way," www.complex.com/music/macklemore-ryan-lewis-interview-2015-cover-story.

Anita Slomski (2014), "Mindfulness-Based Intervention and Substance Abuse Relapse," *Journal of the American Medical Association* 311(24), 2472, http://jamanetwork.com/journals/jama/article-abstract/1883017.

Chapter 8

Please note we are not opposed to medications and believe in certain cases and under the medical direction of a counselor or therapist it may be absolutely essential.

Chapter 9

Stephen Covey, *The 7 Habits of Highly Effective People*, Free Press, 1990.

Stephen Covey, "Habit 5: Seek First to Understand, Then to Be Understood," *The 7 Habits of Highly Effective People*, www.stephencovey.com/7habits/7habits-habit5.php.

Theresa Wiseman (1996), "A Concept Analysis of Empathy," *Journal of Advanced Nursing* 23(16), 1162–67.

Mendez Foundation, Too Good, "Four Attributes of Empathy," October 1, 2015, www.toogoodprograms.org/blog/four-attributes-of-empathy/.

The techniques described in this chapter are known as "Motivational Interviewing." If you'd like to know more, go to the National Library of Medicine, www.ncbi.nlm. nih.gov/books/NBK64964/.

Journal and Workbook
Sheryl Sandberg and Adam Grant, *Option B: Facing Adversity, Building Resilience, and Finding Joy*, Knopf, 2017.

ACKNOWLEDGMENTS

This book would not have been possible without the 300 brave men and women who answered our questions about self-harm and exposed their hearts and souls in our online survey in order to help others heal. To them and our community at HeartSupport, who have opened their lives, we are forever grateful. You are the reason this books exists to help others.

As no book is completed without the efforts of multiple people besides the author, these are the people I want to thank the most.

To the team at HeartSupport:

Jake Luhrs—continued to lead our organization fearlessly and encouraged me when I felt despair producing this book. Nate Hilpert—his voice, edits, and superb recovery knowledge were implemented throughout the entirety of this book. Casey Faris and Dan Bernard—weaved candid stories and helped bring this book to life via video. Megan Huettl—cracked the whip and was always a voice of encouragement. John Williford—put together our marketing efforts and helped distract me with BBQ discourse when I needed it most. Our volunteers—they make the wheels at HeartSupport spin and offer so much encouragement and love to people struggling. Without them, the organization would crumble. Our donors—you're the gas that fuels this mission, and your financial support allowed us to create this book. We cannot thank you enough.

To our Board of Directors:

Dr. Michelle Saari's expert knowledge in mental health and numerous reviews ensured we weren't just making things up that sounded right. Marlis Oliver kept our team on track with his expertise in strategic planning. Finally, Brian Herrman is the reason HeartSupport began many years ago because of his generosity and fervent belief we were essential to a generation.

To our friends and family:

Sandra Wendel gets the first shout out. As my editor, she worked with an insane deadline and provided feedback that took the book to new heights. Without her expertise, the book you've just read would have been a sloppy mess. Peter Voth gets the second one for creating a stellar book cover design.

At the time I wrote this acknowledgment, my wife hadn't read the book. But she patiently endured long nights of my writing and weathered my fits of irritation where I would exclaim, "I'M WRITING! I CANNOT BE DISTURBED!" Her patience, love, and steadfast support as well as allowing me to quit my job, take a pay cut, and work for a nonprofit don't even begin to describe my thanks and love.

When I first began writing, two people influenced me the most—Josh Riebock and Andy Baxter. Josh taught me how to write and lovingly destroyed my first attempts at writing and blogging many years ago, only to help my drafts rise from the ashes. Andy taught me to love words, sentences, books, fantasy, and science fiction. Without these two men, I would still be dreaming about writing.

In a time when everyone else was encouraging their children to get a business degree or doctorate, my family encouraged me to pursue my love of art. To my mom, dad, brother, grandparents, and extended family, thank you for letting me try, fail, and try again to pursue that which I love.

I also want to thank Craig Gross for his initial idea of creating a program to address struggles people in our industry face, and John Burke for his patient years of humility while putting up with a young, punk know-it-all.

Last, and most importantly, as the reformer Martin Luther stated, "*Soli Deo Gloria.*"

ABOUT THE AUTHOR

Benjamin Sledge is the Director of Operations for Heart-Support. Prior to joining the organization, he spent eleven years in the US Army with tours of duty in Iraq and Afghanistan. He is the recipient of a Bronze Star, Purple Heart, and two Army Commendation Medals for his actions overseas.

In addition to his role within the organization, Ben is a voracious reader and writer. He has authored several viral articles that have been featured in numerous publications. While writing is his passion, he dabbles in graphic design (where he received his degree) and leads young adult ministry at his local church. He currently resides in Austin, Texas, with his wife and daughter where he does his part keeping Austin weird by adding to his collection of tattoos.

About the Medical Advisor:

Dr. Michelle Saari sits on the Board of Directors for HeartSupport and has served as a mental health professional for the past fourteen years. She holds both a PhD and master's degree in psychology and is a licensed mental health provider and board-certified clinical supervisor in the state of Minnesota. She is also a Nationally Certified Counselor through the NBCC (National Board for Certified Counselors). She currently works at the Minnesota Department of Corrections where she serves as Director of Psychological Services.

As a longtime fan of the heavy metal music industry, Dr. Saari was aware of the negativity and darkness that many in the scene face. Seeing HeartSupport as a unique blend of the music community, relationship building, and hope for those struggling, she began volunteering on the ground at Vans Warped Tour. She has helped the organization grow to reach even more people while encouraging others to live the healthiest lives they can and discover their best self.

Outside of her professional service, she can be found exploring the outdoors, spending time exercising, and attending as many concerts and music festivals as her schedule allows.

ABOUT HEARTSUPPORT

HeartSupport was created by Grammy-nominated musician Jake Luhrs of metal band August Burns Red. After seeing his fans struggling through the same issues and addictions he went through growing up, he wanted to use his platform to impact a generation.

In 2016, the organization won a Philanthropy Award in recognition of their work at the Alternative Press Music Awards. In 2017, the organization was recognized as one of the Top 100 nonprofits in the world for social innovation.

The team at HeartSupport often travels around United States educating churches, nonprofits, and other organizations, while weaving engaging content along with statistics to inform and train their audiences regarding issues facing today's generation.

JOURNAL

&

WORKBOOK

A note from the author and our mental health advisor:

Before we get started, it's important to understand that this workbook is not meant to provide specific treatment for any condition, diagnosis, or set of symptoms. However, it is meant to increase self-awareness and understanding of self-harm and not replace the work done with a licensed mental health professional. This workbook may also help the reader better communicate their own experience with self-harm while seeking professional advice, working through recovery, or obtaining the support of others. The reader may wish to include exercises from this book into therapy or treatment with a professional, although it is not intended to serve as a replacement.

So with that said, let's put into practice what you've learned so far. For each of the first seven days of this workbook, you'll find an introduction explaining how to complete the questions and what to expect for the day. Each day is different, and the questions will then repeat for the following week to ensure new and healthy habit formation. Each week we'll be working on practicing self-awareness, connecting into community, and building resiliency. That's what you can expect from each day's exercise.

Before you dive in, take a moment to answer these questions. You may recall that in the earlier chapters I stated some of you may feel you're not ready to change. This introduction will help you determine whether or not to proceed now and give you some helpful steps to put in the effort required.

UNDERSTANDING WHY YOU SELF-HARM

Which of these reasons could best explain why you choose to self-harm? You may still be uncertain, but circle the one that resonates with you the most:

- To feel better/physically express emotional pain

- As a method of control

- To feel something other than numbness

- To self-punish

- To distract attention from trauma

What's underneath your reason for choosing that answer? What's important/eye-opening about that discovery for you?

Use this section to write your answers:

AM I READY TO MAKE A CHANGE?

In the chapter on recovery, I discussed that some of you reading this book may not feel ready or even want to change. What can be done then? Here we have some sections for you to write your thoughts to help potentially push you to begin a journey toward healing.

What's the biggest reason that keeps you from being ready to make a change? Maybe some of these reasons can help you process.

Fear (I'm afraid to let go of self-harm)

What are you afraid you would lose if you stopped self-injury? What do you stand to gain by giving up self-harm?

Self-doubt (I don't believe I can actually stop)

Are you afraid of failing? If so, explain why and what you think will happen. What do you think will happen if you never try?

Unwillingness (I don't want to stop)

Take a moment and list all the reasons you think self-harm helps you and brings happiness to your life. After that, list all the bad self-harm does in your life. What did you discover?

Other

Perhaps there's another reason you're not ready to change, but there's always a reason. It's usually hiding under the surface. List as many reasons as you can in this section. Don't even really think about it. Just write whatever comes to mind in an uninterrupted stream of consciousness. It doesn't matter if it seems silly or not.

Use this section to write your answers:

What were some of the thoughts you wrote down? Did any of them help you see a reason why you self-harm? If so, what's that reason? If not, take a day or two and come back to the exercise. Often we have to peel back layers like an onion to get to the root to understand what we're feeling and processing.

If you're like most people, by answering these questions, you'll begin to see there are a lot of negative effects that outweigh the good. Just like when you're driving, there can be blind spots, and you'll need to check those areas to ensure you don't crash.

If you're beginning to see that the negative is outweighing the positive, the only action that can bring about a positive change is to remove self-harm from the equation of your life.

Even if you don't feel ready, just by understanding that there are more negative consequences than positive ones, it's enough to start somewhere in the recovery journey.

We encourage you to continue these practices after the initial three weeks of the workbook and make them a daily habit. By doing so, you can continue to take courageous steps forward and actively see progress.

DAY ONE: COMBATING RESISTANCE

Imagine you're lost in a forest and have no idea where you are. The only advice you've ever heard about getting lost is to begin walking north. Lucky for you, there's a compass in your pack. After hours of walking north using the compass, you find a road you recognize and begin the journey home. Happy ending, right?

Imagine, however, that instead of following that gut feeling about heading north, you decide to find your own way out of the forest. Hours pass and you soon discover you're even more lost. Out of pride you refuse to grab the compass and head north. What do you think will happen?

Today there may be a whole ball of resistance in your gut telling you not to begin these exercises or not to keep doing them. In the same respect, when we experience resistance and choose to give in to its urgings, we're like that person wandering around in the woods too prideful to pull out the compass and head north.

If you'll recall the chapter on recovery, author Steven Pressfield pointed out that resistance is essential to bring about our growth and evolution. The only reason we feel resistance is because we know it's something we must do. Just like a compass that points north, the more resistance you feel around completing these exercises, the more certain you can be that these are the keys that hold the power to break out of your own self-imposed cell.

Resistance is the compass that points true north. When you give in to resistance, it's as if you're heading the opposite direction. Remember that if you didn't hear this voice, these exercises wouldn't be important.

What's the voice of resistance telling you this week? Why is it important to engage against it? *Write your thoughts:*

How do you think or feel you can grow by taking action against the voice of resistance? What happens if you do nothing? How can you make simple steps this week to fight against it?

DAY TWO: OWNING YOUR STORY/THE STORY WE TELL OURSELVES

Suppose your friend told you her amazing life story. When she was ten years old, she was orphaned and forced to live on the streets. One day while she was begging under a nearby bridge, a dark black SUV pulls up and rolls down their window to give your friend a few dollars.

Seeing that it's only a small child, the woman driving takes pity and has your friend climb in the vehicle. At first your friend is resistant, but slowly she begins to trust the woman in the car. After a few weeks she finally takes the woman's offer and is raised as one of the woman's own children.

You sit entranced listening to the story and are amazed at the bravery and difficult conditions your friend faced. But a few months later you discover the truth. The story isn't true. It's completely made up. In fact, your friend has never been orphaned, and her so-called adopted mother turns out to be her biological mother.

When you confront her, she continues to lie, swearing the story she told you is true. When other men and women approach her about the validity of her story, she continues to lie and fabricate even more outlandish claims. Eventually, your friend becomes utterly convinced the lie she tells is reality because she refuses to face the facts.

In this situation, how would you feel? Betrayed? Sorry for your friend? Pity?

133 | The Middle

When we refuse to own the parts of our story, we become like the girl in the story, inventing a happier and more wishful version we tell ourselves to keep us in denial about the reality of the situation we're in. Perhaps we think we can control our self-harm. That no one needs to know. Or perhaps the story we tell ourselves is that we're worthless and deserve this.

Either way, we're in denial and not owning up to many aspects of our own story. Today, we'll examine the power of your weekly story and why it's important to write it correctly each week.

Just like the girl in the story, each of us tells ourselves stories that are untrue (such as "No one will ever love me." "I'm a failure in life." "All my friends hate me.") What's the story you're telling yourself? What aspects are real? Which ones are false?

In your own current story, there will be moments that shine in your memory. Which parts of your story so far are you proud to embrace? Why? Which parts are difficult to embrace? Why?

What's the pattern you notice between what you choose to embrace and what you don't? Which parts are more imagined than real?

Are you sharing your story with someone currently to own the true parts and combat the lies? If you haven't yet, choose a trusted friend who's read this book or understands empathetic listening. You can even choose a counselor to begin this conversation with. Remember, we cannot experience empathy if we're not connecting in community.

DAY THREE: FIGHTING SHAME AND DEVELOPING A RESILIENT SPIRIT

If you've ever seen a movie in which people are in a military boot camp or an intense fitness boot camp, you've watched the instructors scream, "You're pathetic! Faster, maggot!" or something along those lines.

In this book, I pointed out that nothing productive has ever been associated with shame messages. Yet, in the military and fitness boot camps, men and women seem to have the opposite happen, right? They develop mental grit, endure hardship, and form camaraderie. What's the reasoning behind this?

As a group, the men and women in training have a common enemy: the drill instructor or the fitness guru. As they're torn down, they encourage and carry one another. After a while they even begin to poke fun at their drill sergeants. When they're forced to run, they do so singing cadence. When they're tired and the instructor claims they can't finish, they prove them wrong and throw it in the leader's face.

By the end of their training, the taunts and insults roll off them like rain, and they're stronger, faster, and more agile, proving to their instructors they have what it takes.

In short, they've developed mental grit and resilience. They can hear the disparaging messages and know they're not true and understand how to fight against them.

Each week you'll engage the messages that yell at you like a drill sergeant telling you you're worthless and pathetic and develop the resilience necessary to combat it. Shame will become your common enemy.

So if you're ready, welcome to your boot camp.

What are some of the most common characteristics, triggers, or patterns you experience when you feel shame? What is the message they tell you and where (or when) did you first start believing them? *Write them here:*

Remember shame tells us "I am bad. I am worthless. I deserve this," and other similar messages. Imagine for a moment your best friend comes to you saying these things about herself. What would you say to your friend to convince her otherwise? Why? Write that down:

Now imagine what she (or he) would say to you if you shared that you feel worthless. Would you believe her? Why or why not?

Shame messages trick us into believing the worst about ourselves. Write out true statements that your best friend, a family member you know who loves you, or a higher power would use to describe you. What keeps you from believing the loving things they would say about you?

Are you talking about how you feel and asking for what you need from others when you feel shame? Who is someone you can reach out to this week to share what you're feeling? Feel free to write additional thoughts here as well.

DAY FOUR: YOUR ENVIRONMENT AND RELATIONSHIPS

In college, I ended up in one of the most toxic relationships I can remember. A girl I liked strung me along like a pet, only to discard me when she got bored. My relationship and the environment we spent time in were completely unhealthy. My friends thought she was pretty and would encourage me to stay with her. She would go back to her games, and I would get fed up and distance myself. Months down the road I'd miss her or she'd call, and then I was right back to being miserable.

One summer I fell back into her grasp, after we reconnected. We planned a weekend getaway together at the lake with a group of mutual friends. The only problem was I got immediately ditched and found out she'd been on a boat all day with a bunch of other guys. As a response, I began hanging around another girl I knew liked me. The weekend culminated in an epic display of pure relational toxicity when we both ended up jealous and angry. I got slapped, only to make up and make out in a parking lot.

My friends convinced me it was time to cut ties after that event, and she and I didn't talk for close to a year afterward.

One evening I saw her in a restaurant and we began to catch up. We laughed and carried on while the flirting got pretty intense. Once I came to my senses, I decided it was time to leave before things got worse. She walked me to my car and hugged me only to whisper that I should come back to her house. When I responded, "I have a girlfriend," her response was, "She doesn't have to know."

In your own story, the environment and relationships you're in might just be keeping you in the same cycles of self-harm without your realizing it. Just like me, maybe it's someone you feel you can't say no to or don't know how to escape the cycle. In this section, we'll take a look at everything from your community to the environment you're in.

Relationships, circumstances, events, and times of year all play into your environment and what's going on around you. What feeling do you have the most right before you want to self-harm?

List the top five places/circumstances/relationships/ people that trigger you:

1. _____

2. _____

3. _____

4. _____

5. _____

List the emotion it triggers that causes you to want to self-harm:

1. _____

2. _____

3. _____

4. _____

5. _____

Now list potential solutions to each environment:

1. _____

2. _____

3. _____

4. _____

5. _____

What trends did you notice within the triggers and your feelings? Are there unhealthy relationships, friendships, or places you need to cut ties with? What would keep you from doing so? *Note: If you live at home with your parents and they're a triggering environment, think about safe places you can spend time in when you're not in school or work. That can be with friends, a church, or volunteering somewhere.*

Who are the people who can help you to take action and break free from this environment? Can you identify someone you want as a mentor or a friend who can help you? It's important to note they should be mature or older if you're looking for a mentor.

Take a step and reach out to that person this week. *If you don't know where to turn,* we'd love for you to join the community at HeartSupport. **Visit heartsupport.com/ community to learn more.**

DAY FIVE: INSPIRATION

Have you ever been inspired by a movie?

Some people remember the first time they saw Star Wars or the Avengers. Maybe when you were a child you wanted to fly and be a beacon of hope for others after reading the Superman comics. Maybe there's a book you've read that changed the way you view life or even a favorite song that resonates deeply with you.

There's a good chance in each of these examples you can quote a line or lyric from your favorites. We need others to inspire us toward greatness. We want to believe humans can fly, the impossible can happen, and love conquers darkness.

Today's exercise is simple. We've drawn from our favorite inspirational quotes and have some questions for you to answer to leave you feeling empowered.

> Whatever you do, you need courage. Whatever course you decide upon, there is always someone to tell you that you are wrong. There are always difficulties arising that tempt you to believe your critics are right. To map out a course of action and follow it to an end requires some of the same courage that a soldier needs. Peace has its victories, but it takes brave men and women to win them.
> —Ralph Waldo Emerson

Right now, you're in the middle of a battle with self-harm and it may be hard to muster courage. There may even be critics telling you it's hopeless. But courage is contagious. Write down a story of one of the most courageous things you've seen happen. Why was it courageous? In what ways were you inspired by that person's actions? What small, courageous step can you take today? *Write your answers on the next page*

DAY SIX: SERVICE AND DISTRACTION

The day I came home from Iraq was one of the loneliest days of my life. I had no one to pick me up at the airport, and I didn't know how to get to the new house where I was supposed to be living.

My wife had filed for divorce a month earlier while I was overseas.

The pain of that event landed me on my best friend's couch. A month later, I would get my own apartment and a cat. Kasey, my cat, was like Wilson the volleyball from the Tom Hanks movie Cast Away—a friend to talk to, which helped take away the pangs of loneliness.

After some time I got involved at my local church volunteering with teenagers. It was there I made some of my very best friends and moved from isolation to connectedness. Another thing happened I didn't expect. My boredom, loneliness, and rampant drinking began to fade. I was so busy volunteering, I didn't have time to stay stuck in harmful scenarios. I was completely distracted by the amount of responsibility and fun I was having.

Serving in shared experiences will help you find people who enjoy similar passions. Do you enjoy music and concerts? Consider volunteering at a large festival. Do you enjoy writing like I do? Writing helped me find other writers and get my work published (and I was horrible when I began).

Choosing a service area that aligns with your interests can be extremely beneficial to your recovery because it not only motivates you to do something besides injuring, but can provide a welcome distraction.

List five activities you're passionate about. It could range from learning to play an instrument to a love for animals.

1. _____

2. _____

3. _____

4. _____

5. _____

Can you pursue any of these when you feel the urge to self-harm? What can you volunteer to do? (*For instance, if you love animals, then walk dogs at an animal shelter.*) What step will you take toward trying out an activity this week? Who will you tell to encourage you and hold you responsible?

Weekly distraction idea: Try to begin learning a new skill you've wanted to try out for a while. Whether that's learning to code or starting to write (all the information you need is free and online to do so). *Use the space here to write any additional thoughts.*

DAY SEVEN: CRITICAL AWARENESS, REFLECTION, AND CELEBRATION

Let's say you know someone who comes from a wealthy family and decides to throw a birthday bash. Upon arriving at the party, you can hardly believe your eyes. There are white-gloved waiters serving your favorite food. A section of the backyard has a dance floor with one of your favorite bands playing. The pool is multilevel and almost resembles a water park. Then comes time to cut the cake and open presents.

After all the presents have been opened, your friend stands and exclaims, "This is it? I only got 70 percent of what I wanted! This is crap!"

What would you think? Probably that your friend is a spoiled brat who's unappreciative.

We can experience the same pitfalls when we don't practice critical awareness and celebrate our small victories. Say, for instance, this week has been the greatest progress you've made in your battle with self-harm. Instead of injuring four times a week, you only injured once. To say, "I still injured 25 percent of the time! This is crap!" is not practicing the critical realization you injured much less than normal. Instead of reflecting and celebrating, you set yourself up for failure instead of seeing the amazing amount of hard work you've put in.

Far too often we think that in order to make a change it has to be a 180-degree turn. However, a 1-degree change is still a turn in the right direction, and when you eventually add enough of them up they become 180 1-degree turns.

Take some time for reflection to practice critical awareness. What's going on in your life currently? What is a
good thing that happened this week? What's been disappointing? Where can you slowly improve? *Journal your
thoughts here:*

Reflect on the progress made this week and celebrate anything from a tiny victory to a large one. Write down that win here:

Who or what can you thank this week to practice gratitude for taking small steps? Why?

Celebrate the days (or hours) you didn't injure

Day 1	Day 2	Day 3	Day 4	Day 5	Day 6	Day 7

DAY EIGHT: COMBATING RESISTANCE

What's the voice of resistance telling you this week? Why is it important to engage against it? *Write your thoughts:*

How do you think or feel you can grow by taking action against the voice of resistance this week? What happens if you do nothing? How can you make simple steps this week to fight against it?

DAY NINE: OWNING YOUR STORY/THE STORY WE TELL OURSELVES

What's the story you're telling yourself today? What aspects are real? Which ones are false?

[blank box]

Which parts of your story and the progress you've made are you proud to embrace? Why? Which parts have been difficult to embrace? Why?

[blank box]

Are there any patterns you're noticing this week between what you choose to embrace and what you don't? Which parts are more imagined than real?

Who do you plan to share your story with this week to own the true parts and combat the lies? What do you think they'll tell you?

DAY TEN: FIGHTING SHAME AND DEVELOPING A RESILIENT SPIRIT

What are some of the most common characteristics, triggers, or patterns you've been experiencing when you feel shame? What is the message they're telling you this week? *Write them here:*

In their book, *Option B: Facing Adversity, Building Resilience and Finding Joy,* Adam Grant and Sheryl Sandberg explain:

"We plant the seeds of resilience in the ways we process negative events. After spending decades studying how people deal with setbacks, psychologist Martin Seligman found that three P's can stunt recovery: (1) personalization—the belief that we are at fault; (2) pervasiveness—the belief that an event will affect all areas of our life; and (3) permanence—the belief that the aftershocks of the event will last forever. The three P's play like the flip side of the pop song 'Everything Is Awesome'—'everything is awful.' The loop in your head repeats, 'It's my fault this is awful. My whole life is awful. And it's always going to be awful.'"

What steps can you take this week to combat the "three P's" and process negative events in a positive light or different manner?

Write out true statements that your best friend, a family member you know who loves you, or a higher power would use to describe you. What keeps you from believing the loving things they would say about you?

Are you talking about how you feel and asking for what you need from others when you feel shame? Who is someone you can reach out to this week to share what you're feeling?

DAY ELEVEN: YOUR ENVIRONMENT AND RELATIONSHIPS

What feeling do you have the most right before you want to self-harm?

List the top five places/circumstances/relationships/people that may have triggered you this last week:

1. _____

2. _____

3. _____

4. _____

5. _____

List the emotion it triggers that causes you to want to self-harm:

1. _____

2. _____

3. _____

4. _____

5. _____

Now list potential solutions to each environment:

1. _____

2. _____

3. _____

4. _____

5. _____

What trends did you notice within the triggers and your feelings? What's different from last week? Are there areas or situations you need to cut ties with? If so, what's stopping you?

Who can help you this week to take action and break free from this environment? Why would you choose them?

If you don't know where to turn, you can always use the community at HeartSupport. **Visit heartsupport.com/ community to learn more.**

DAY TWELVE: INSPIRATION

Strength and courage aren't always measured in medals and victories. They are measured in the struggles they overcome. The strongest people aren't always the people who win, but the people who don't give up when they lose.
—Ashley Hodgeson

Maybe you relapsed. Maybe today is hard. Winning isn't everything, but the small strides forward are what count. Write about a time you failed something (a test, losing in a championship game, etc). What happened afterwards? What did you learn? Did you become stronger? *Write your answers on the following page.*

DAY THIRTEEN: SERVICE AND DISTRACTION

What steps have you taken to volunteer or pursue a passion? If you haven't, what's stopped you from doing so? Have you tried to implement doing these activities when you feel the urge to self-injure? What's been the result?

What step will you take toward trying out an activity this week? Who will you tell to encourage you and hold you responsible?

Weekly distraction idea: Invite a friend out for a meal or coffee to catch up. If it's the weekend, consider going camping with them!

DAY FOURTEEN: CRITICAL AWARENESS, REFLECTION, AND CELEBRATION

Take some time for reflection to practice critical awareness. What's going on in your life currently? What is a
good thing that happened this week? What's been disappointing? Where can you slowly improve? *Journal your
thoughts here:*

Reflect on the progress made this week and celebrate anything from a tiny victory to a large one. Write down that win here:

Who or what can you thank this week to practice gratitude for taking small steps? Why?

Celebrate the days (or hours) you didn't injure

Day 8	Day 9	Day 10	Day 11	Day 12	Day 13	Day 14

DAY FIFTEEN: COMBATING RESISTANCE

What's the voice of resistance telling you this week? Why is it important to engage against it? *Write your thoughts:*

How do you think or feel you can grow by taking action against the voice of resistance this week? What happens if you do nothing? How can you make simple steps this week to fight against it?

DAY SIXTEEN: OWNING YOUR STORY/THE STORY WE TELL OURSELVES

What's the story you're telling yourself today? What aspects are real? Which ones are false?

Which parts of your story and the progress you've made are you proud to embrace? Why? Which parts have been difficult to embrace? Why?

Are there any patterns you're noticing this week between what you choose to embrace and what you don't? Which parts are more imagined than real?

Who do you plan to share your story with this week to own the true parts and combat the lies? What do you think they'll tell you?

DAY SEVENTEEN: FIGHTING SHAME AND DEVELOPING A RESILIENT SPIRIT

What are some of the most common characteristics, triggers, or patterns you've been experiencing when you feel shame? What is the message they're telling you this week? *Write them here:*

Reflect on the 'three P's" from the previous week— personalization—the belief that we are at fault; (2) pervasiveness—the belief that an event will affect all areas of our life; and (3) permanence—the belief that the aftershocks of the event will last forever. What steps can you take this week to combat the "three P's" and process negative events in a positive light or different manner?

Write out true statements that your best friend, a family member you know who loves you, or a higher power would use to describe you. What keeps you from believing the loving things they would say about you?

Are you talking about how you feel and asking for what you need from others when you feel shame? Who is someone you can reach out to this week to share what you're feeling? *Write out any additional thoughts here.*

DAY EIGHTEEN: YOUR ENVIRONMENT AND RELATIONSHIPS

What feeling do you have the most right before you want to self-harm?

List the top five places/circumstances/relationships/ people that may have triggered you this last week:

1. _____

2. _____

3. _____

4. _____

5. _____

List the emotion it triggers that causes you to want to self-harm:

1. _____

2. _____

3. _____

4. _____

5. _____

Now list potential solutions to each environment:

1. _____

2. _____

3. _____

4. _____

5. _____

What trends did you notice within the triggers and your feelings? What's different from last week? Are there areas or situations you need to cut ties with? If so, what's stopping you?

Who can help you this week to take action and break free from this environment? Why would you choose them?

If you don't know where to turn, you can always use the community at HeartSupport. **Visit heartsupport.com/ community to learn more.**

DAY NINETEEN: INSPIRATION

If children with terminal cancer can find love, joy, beauty and peace in their day – and they do – why don't we?
— Dan Zadra

Sometimes we're so focused on the things that are going horribly in our life, that we miss the beauty of little things. Where can you find beauty and inspiration this week? What are the small but comforting moments you've experienced? Even if things are hard, what's something you saw this week that moved you?

DAY TWENTY: SERVICE AND DISTRACTION

What steps have you taken to volunteer or pursue a passion? If you haven't, what's stopped you from doing so? Have you tried to implement doing these activities when you feel the urge to self-injure? What's been the result?

What step will you take toward trying out an activity this week? Who will you tell to encourage you and hold you responsible?

Weekly distraction idea: Do something physical this week! When you exercise your body releases endorphins, which triggers a positive feeling. Consider running a few miles (or just a mile), walking, crossfit, going to a gym, yoga, or even exercising in a park. If you feel the urge this week, go exercise instead and then come back and write how you feel after!

DAY TWENTY-ONE: CRITICAL AWARENESS, REFLECTION, AND CELEBRATION

Take some time for reflection to practice critical awareness. What's going on in your life currently? What is a good thing that happened this week? What's been disappointing? Where can you slowly improve? *Journal your thoughts here:*

Reflect on the progress made this week and celebrate anything from a tiny victory to a large one. Write down that win here:

Who or what can you thank this week to practice gratitude for taking small steps? Why?

Celebrate the days (or hours) you didn't injure

Day 15	Day 16	Day 17	Day 18	Day 19	Day 20	Day 21

FAMILY

&

FRIENDS SECTION

When you first discovered your loved one was self-harming, what was your immediate reaction (your feelings and thoughts)? *Write everything here to process:*

Now that you have your thoughts and feelings on paper, the goal is to understand why you reacted that way. Often our reaction comes from both a genuine place of compassion but also from hurts we've experienced in our own past and the beliefs we formed as a result. Far too often we want to fix people and keep them from making the same mistakes we have, and thus feel it's a reflection of us instead.

The following questions will help you process and release you from the responsibility you may feel to fix the situation and instead walk alongside your loved one or friend toward healing.

Looking back at your initial reaction, which part had more to do with you and less with them? How do you feel their injuring reflects on your worth as a parent/ supporter/friend (in other words, "I'd be embarrassed to share this with others because it makes me look like a bad parent/friend," or "I was hurt they hid this behavior from me")?

Do you feel the need to defend or fix her? Do you feel hurt that he didn't tell you or perhaps he hasn't taken your advice? If so, why?

What do you fear will happen if this self-injury doesn't stop? Fill in the blank here and then answer the question.

My greatest fear is that their self-harm means I

_____

_____

_____

(example: failed as a parent or friend, aren't good enough, lack the skills to help). What does this say to you?

Look back over your answers and see where it's become more about your identity than being emotional first aid for someone else. It's okay that some of your answers may appear less than noble. In fact, we've seen it firsthand in our own team at HeartSupport.

One member of our team, Nate, was helping one of his friends through his drug-addiction recovery. He invited his friend to stay with him for nine months and did everything he could to encourage his recovery. He invited his friend to meetings, helped him find a sponsor, helped him develop his faith, and was there for him in the moments he needed a friend.

After nine months of helping, Nate left to go on Vans Warped Tour to help other men and women struggling, only to discover his friend had relapsed, robbed his apartment, and disappeared. Originally, Nate was furious, but mostly at himself because he felt as if he had failed. He felt there was something more he could have done.

A mentor of his offered a different perspective one day, however; and it cut to Nate's core. What he told Nate was this: "You wanted his sobriety more than he did."

What Nate realized is that recovery and healing is a choice that has to be made within the individual and can't be put into them, no matter how hard you try. He realized that if he spent less time trying to recover *for* his friend and more time helping his friend understand why he struggled to take ownership himself, he might have been able to offer more effective help.

Right now, you may want your friend or child's sobriety from self-harm more than they do. The question we need to ask you is whether you're willing to let your loved one or friend make their own choices even if it means they fail and experience more pain? Can you focus on listening and understanding instead of correcting until your loved one wants freedom from self-harm for themselves?

Remember that in our section about listening, we relayed that *feeling heard* is so close to *feeling loved* that they're almost inseparable. The key is to focus on seeing the world through their eyes and trying to understand why *they* see things the way they do.

Here are a few scenarios that you may experience and some practice word tracks to help you begin to listen and offer emotional first aid. If you need a refresher, reread the listening section in the chapter on friends and family who want to help. Remember that evaluating, probing, advising, and interpreting are not effective means of listening, but listening to understand *is*. We've offered an initial section to show you the wrong, and right way to listen. After, you'll have a chance to write out the wrong, and write ways to listen in a few more exercises.

"I really just don't want to talk about it."

Evaluating: Well, that's not helpful to just shut down like that.

Probing: Why not? You know you can trust me. Give me a chance! What's going on?

Advising: Well, you should open up because it's going to help you get rid of your shame.

Interpreting: I know just how you feel, but when I was struggling, I had to let that go. You do too.

Listening to Understand: It's scary to talk about what you're feeling. You don't want to open up to me just to be judged and hurt more.

"Exactly. I just don't know if I can trust you."

Evaluating:

Probing:

Advising:

Interpreting:

Listening to Understand:

"You always tell me I'm doing something wrong."

Evaluating:

Probing:

Advising:

Interpreting:

Listening to Understand:

"You just won't understand."

Evaluating:

Probing:

Advising:

Interpreting:

Listening to Understand:

"I've been cutting for six months."

Evaluating:

Probing:

Advising:

Interpreting:

Listening to Understand:

"I'm afraid I can't stop, and I don't know what to do."

Evaluating:

Probing:

Advising:

Interpreting:

Listening to Understand:

"I really want to get better, but I'm afraid I won't be able to."

Evaluating:

Probing:

Advising:

Interpreting:

Listening to Understand:

Remember: listening takes practice. In your whole life, how many courses have you taken on writing or speaking? How many have you taken on listening? The difference is clear: we are not taught how to listen well. But we can learn.

ALSO FROM HEARTSUPPORT

Join band members from August Burns Red, Black Veil Brides, We Came As Romans, Memphis May Fire, Miss May I, and Blessthefall as they teach you how to:

- Take back your life from the control of anxiety and depression
- Heal from the roots for lasting change
- Finally break old habits with help from experts

Learn more at heartsupport.com/restore

97106735R00109

Made in the USA
Columbia, SC
07 June 2018